Shock: shok a violent impact, *orig* of charging warriors; a dashing together; a shaking or unsettling blow ... a convulsive excitation of nerves; to shake or impair by a shock. *Adj (journalism)* sensational, surprising, unexpected, as in *a shock result.*

The Chambers Dictionary

Lorne Gardner has spent 25 years in sports journalism – almost exclusively with the *Scottish Daily Mail* and *Mail on Sunday* where he served as head of sport until October 2020. Following a short spell with DC Thomson, he was appointed sports editor of *The Times Scotland* in June 2021.

For Siobhan, Joe, Sam and Eve.
Without their support I'd have given up long ago.

1971

WHAT A SENSATION

50 YEARS ON FROM THE DAY PARTICK THISTLE SHOCKED THE WORLD OF FOOTBALL

LORNE GARDNER

DB PUBLISHING

CONTENTS

CHAPTER ONE

THE INTRODUCTION

'We want people to come and watch us not just because they have a soft spot for Thistle but because we are a go-ahead successful team. We want to be worth watching.' – Davie McParland

IT'S not easy being a fan of Partick Thistle. Supporters of this Maryhill institution have heard and been the butt of many a joke – from end-of-the-pier shows to Billy Connolly and *Still Game*. Our team is often described as eccentric and the great unpredictables – a side capable of hitting magnificent highs one week and catastrophic lows the next. And when we confirm our allegiances to any grand inquisitor we are almost always immediately asked, 'Aye, but who do you really support?'

Let me nail my colours to the mast here and now. Partick Thistle has been my club since that very first match I attended as a kid. I recall with great clarity climbing up the steps inside the old stand, looking out over a Firhill bathed in sunshine and being mesmerised by the spectacle and colour of it all. We played Aberdeen that day – don't ask me what the result was, although I'm sure I could hazard a guess.

Let me also be honest and admit that I have never bought a season ticket, that I miss the odd home game and that my desire to travel to watch them on away days has dwindled and diminished over the years. That being said, I have stood behind the goal at Alloa, watched them at Forfar while leaning on the roof of the away dugout and even stood on the battlements of Dumbarton Castle with my mate Ronnie to watch them play at The Rock below. As I recall we were beaten 2-0.

So I may not be Partick Thistle's most loyal supporter, but I'll follow them through thin and thin; draw, lose or draw. They have given me moments of great joy and heartbreaking disappointment, been the source of heated debate with both of my sons, my brothers and my nephew (all of whom are similarly afflicted) and fuelled laughter and tears in equal measure.

It is also not stretching the point too far to say Thistle were there for me in my hour of need.

Up until October 2020 I was in a job I not only loved but obsessed over. I need not go into too much detail other than to say that after 25 years I assumed, wrongly as it turned out, that I would be there until I decided it was time to go. I never saw redundancy as a possibility but as a boxer will tell you, it is not the punches you see coming that hurt, it's the ones you don't. Suddenly, a word that meant very little to anyone just months before had decided my immediate future: Covid.

I was in shock for weeks. I wouldn't wish that feeling of rejection on my worst enemy – nor the feeling of failure that accompanied each and every rejected job application.

With little but lockdown to occupy my time, I met up with an old pal who, in an almost throwaway line, reminded me that 2021 was to be a special year for Thistle – the centenary of the Scottish Cup win over Rangers and the 50th anniversary of the League Cup triumph over Celtic. We chatted about that for no more than a few minutes but it must have put a grain, the tiniest scintilla, of an idea into my head. The next day, as is usual with me, that tiny germ of an idea fell front and centre in my mind. Why not use the time I now found myself with to pen the definitive account of that 1971 success? Why not tell the story of the players and people involved in the greatest shock Scottish football has ever witnessed?

So that is what I set out to do. And that is why I maintain the club saved me. By helping me fill the endless hours of lockdown after lockdown by giving me a purpose and a project. By giving me a passion.

I believe, and I of course admit I am biased, that Thistle's triumph over Celtic that day has never been given the credit it deserves as Scottish football's greatest upset. And I can make a case to back up my argument.

Let us look at the evidence.

Firstly, the Celtic team Thistle faced that day – if they were not already legends they would soon achieve such status. Tommy Gemmell, Bobby Murdoch, Jimmy Johnstone and Jim Craig had all been part of the Lisbon Lions, the first British team to lift the European Cup just three seasons earlier. They had lost the European Cup Final to Feyenoord in 1970, a game they should have won. And they had reached the quarter-finals of the same competition a matter of months prior to facing Thistle. They also had a stunningly talented new crop of players emerging, such as the likes of Lou Macari, Davie Hay and Kenny Dalglish. They were all part of what became known as the Quality Street Gang, a sparkling collection of youngsters being nurtured in the east end of Glasgow. Significantly, they were also in the process of an historic nine-in-a-row title run.

Secondly, there was the Celtic manager, Jock Stein. If Sir Alex Ferguson talks of Stein as the greatest then who am I to argue? Words such as 'legend' are thrown around too easily in football. But there is no other way of describing the man. Nor is there any way of possibly exaggerating his influence on Scottish, and British, football.

Thirdly, let us look at Thistle. A youthful team for whom many had been playing reserve football just a season before. Half of the players were part-time. Denis McQuade was a student, Frank Coulston a PE teacher, and Jimmy Bone worked in the pits. They had just bounced back from the first relegation in their history, managed by a 36-year-old Davie McParland who was only 18 months in the job by the time the final came.

Nobody gave Thistle a chance that day. There were even elements within the Thistle team who believed they would be beaten, albeit that they would not go down without a fight.

Archie Macpherson, who was at Hampden that October day and who kindly gave up his time to be interviewed for this book, agrees.

'It is the biggest shock I can recall,' he told me. 'It was a final, against a team that seemed indomitable, they could still have that aura of European champions about them and they were humbled. It wasn't a fluke goal. I can't think of anything, quite a stunning reversal of predictions. That stands out.'

What happened that day, and specifically in the opening 40 minutes of the match, sent shockwaves across the world of football.

It is interesting that when I got involved in conversation with people and told them I was writing this book, they could all remember where they were that day of 23 October 1971. And almost without fail they recall hearing the half-time score and refusing to believe it.

So, this is the story of the greatest day in the history of Partick Thistle Football Club, told by the people who were there. It is not a potted history of that season. It does not deal in statistics or make much mention of how the season had unfolded before that day at Hampden. My initial idea was to contain the book to the day itself, the 24 hours from dawn to dusk. That plan evolved over time and conversations with those involved. But it does not go much further back than the quarter-final success over St Johnstone and touches only really in passing on what happened after the final.

What I wanted was to tell the human stories of those who were eye-witnesses to history, not the history of my beloved club. Others are far more qualified than me to do that.

I was anxious that any book must have the backing of the club so I approached first Brian Welsh and then CEO Gerry Britton who were both immediately receptive to the idea. Gerry in turn took the proposal to the board who welcomed it unanimously. I thank each and every one of them for their support and guidance.

Off and running, it was then a question of interviewing as many people as possible, which included each member of the team. To a man each of the boys of '71 was a gem to work with, helpful and accommodating and so happy to talk over old times. I can't thank them enough for their help, especially when I returned to them endlessly with that Columbo question, 'Ah, just one more thing!'

I would also like to thank Celtic legends Davie Hay and Jim Craig who agreed to recount their side of the story despite playing on the losing team that day.

Special mention must also be made for Davie McParland's daughter Yvonne who spoke so eloquently about her father, a legend to all Thistle fans but to her simply Dad. It is sad that, as we talk about the 50th anniversary of the club's greatest day, the man who inspired it is no longer with us.

I have used what they told me and wrapped it in a narrative, a story of that day and the build-up to it, adding background and colour to weave their tale. I hope they forgive me that use of artistic licence. The comments and quotes from Davie come from interviews he gave at the time.

I also must pay special thanks to Stuart Deans, whose encyclopaedic knowledge of all things Thistle was a great asset and the cuttings he was able to supply a constant source of information. I can't thank him enough.

Several times during the process I realised that writing a book is a daunting responsibility. It's not the fact-checking, of which there was much and if any errors have slipped through the net I apologise. Nor the fact that the memory can play tricks on you over the passing of five decades. What worried me most was that I was telling the story of the boys of '71. A story I believe that has never been told before and one which I think unfairly has never been given the credit it deserves. I was telling their tale and I wanted to get it right. I wanted to do them justice. I hope I have achieved that.

You, dear reader, can decide whether or not I succeeded.

'Somehow McParland put together a combination of young guys and old guys and created something special,' defender John Hansen told me.

'I think before the game Celtic thought they just had to turn up and didn't realise we didn't have anything to lose. I think they were used to maybe teams playing against them and being intimidated and playing defensively and trying to hold out. And they were just taken aback with us and just couldn't cope. 'We didn't realise, and probably Stein didn't realise, that a lot of that Celtic team were coming to the end. They didn't realise that they were going to be open to young guys attacking them not knowing any better than just attack. Before they knew it, they were 4-0 down and couldn't find a way back. Sometimes things like that happen. You could replay that match 100 times and it wouldn't happen like that again.

'But it did, and it changed our lives forever.'

This is their story.

Lorne Gardner
March 2021

CHAPTER 2

THE MANAGER

THE café in Milngavie was bustling, the noisy chatter and the clinking of crockery carrying out into the street. The congregation was engrossed in their conversations; the gossip, catching up with news about friends and family. Davie McParland sat at his table quietly mulling over a pot of tea and waiting for his friend to arrive.

His mind was on football. Newly appointed to his role as Partick Thistle manager, he had been tasked with picking up the pieces of the catastrophic season before – which had seen the team relegated for the first time.

Scot Symon had been removed from the manager's chair after failing to arrest the worrying decline. Relegation had been confirmed with defeat at home to Dundee United by the end of March and the final games of the 1969/70 season had been spent fretting about what would happen next.

Robert Reid, who would go on to hold almost every administrative role at the club in the years to follow, had travelled with Symon to a reserve match just as the season was plummeting towards its conclusion.

'I remember he turned to me and asked, "Robert, tell me something, what do the fans think about me?" Reid said.

'Now that was a very, very difficult question for me to answer. I don't remember how I managed to skirt around that but frankly Scot's time was up. To be honest he had run out of the ability, the energy, the drive to manage a football team.'

But Reid was still worried. The early campaign in the Second Division had been pockmarked with defeats to Clydebank, Brechin and Albion Rovers. It was hardly the kind of form to fuel a promotion back to the top flight. As he entered the café and sat down opposite McParland, the conversation turned to his concerns.

'I remember I was absolutely distraught,' said Reid. 'Here we were, relegated, not winning in the lower division.'

Reid recalls McParland's response clearly.

'He told me not to worry,' Reid said. 'It would just take time and he explained to me to relax, all will be well.'

'And he was right, it turned out absolutely fine. Now we had a lot of very good, young players, don't get me wrong, but they were not quite ready. So, we blended the experience of Hugh Strachan and Alex Rae to this emerging talent and it took off almost immediately.'

'We went on to the top division.'

In fact, Thistle didn't lose a home game all season – 16 wins and two draws as McParland put his faith in young players like Alan Rough, John Hansen, Alex Forsyth, Denis McQuade, Johnny Gibson and others, and trusted the influence of Alex Rae, Hugh Strachan, Frank Coulston and Jackie Campbell.

Such faith would take Thistle all the way to Hampden.

'He wasn't on the park but if he hadn't been the manager we wouldn't have won the cup,' said John Hansen. 'It was down to him and the way he organised us and the way he got us playing. He didn't try to weigh us down on the day with new tactics – it was just go out and play.'

* * *

McPARLAND has swapped his usual sartorial elegance for the tracksuit. He is a hands-on manager. A complete change from his predecessor. At only 36 years of age, he is young to be in the role but he is a Thistle legend, a one-club man of 587 games and 110 goals.

'It was a totally different way of working under McParland than it had been under Scot Symon,' said Jackie Campbell, one of the experienced heads retained in the team. 'Symon was an old-school manager. He didn't take much to do with the training, he left a lot of that to the coaches, but McParland was the tracksuit manager on the training field. It was totally different.

'He was more hands-on. He would take you out on to the pitch and lay it out, how he wanted you to play and what he wanted from you. He was a coach whereas the older managers weren't really coaches. So that was a transition for Thistle.'

McParland has a determined, ruthless streak but it is what the club needs after the first relegation in its history. He knew what he had to do when the Thistle board made the decision to thrust him into the job. There was too much dead wood within the squad and a deep reservoir of young talent bursting through the reserves, itching for their chance. They were raw, rough around the edges, but McParland could see their stunning potential. All he needed was time, an opportunity for them to flourish, and a couple of old heads to show them the way.

The climb back to the top flight had been completed with relative ease despite the initial teething problems. The opening league game of the new campaign could not have gone better. In front of a Firhill crowd of 27,000, McParland had watched his side, inspired by the gifted Johnny Gibson, sweep aside the mighty Rangers 3-2. Gibson in fact had been unplayable that day – two goals in the first half before he had to leave the action because of an injury. Combined with a winning start to the League Cup campaign, everything in Maryhill is on the up. People are beginning to notice.

McParland gives an interview to newspaper reporters.

'Our season "downstairs" was one thing Thistle would not like to repeat,' he says. 'And yet in retrospect it certainly didn't do the club any harm.

'Relegation hit us hard. Make no mistake. But at that particular time at Firhill it was probably one of the best things that could have happened.

'Young players had a season to learn more about their trade in a less demanding division. We were able to experiment in several situations, build for the future.

'And at the end of it all, with hard work from everybody from the boardroom to the ground staff, we succeeded in getting back in a year.

'I am sure we have come back a better and more organised team. Not just because of that one result against Rangers. Being successful in the big league is as hard as trying to find a parking meter in the city centre. It is a tremendous challenge. Yet Thistle must think positively. By that I mean I know what we want and know exactly what we are prepared to do.'

His players know exactly what they can get away with and, more importantly, what they can't. Many of them owe McParland a debt. For not only did he hand them their chance, he stuck by them. If that means abiding by his strict nature then it is a price worth paying. A roll and bacon in Jaconelli's beside Firhill after training is fine. But don't push it.

'He was a father figure more than anything else,' said Alan Rough. 'I had been at Thistle since I was 16, come through the under-16 team and then went to Sighthill Amateurs, which was a sort of pre-reserve side with Eddie McCulloch. It was a progression of players from there into the reserves so Davie knew me when I was only 16.

'He was always watching what you were doing. He was old-school, like Jock Stein. He knew where you were at the weekend, he knew you'd been down at Jaconelli's. He was one of those guys who knew everything and it was a good thing because it kept you in your place.'I only played about three or four junior games before I went into the reserves. I remember him saying to me, "Junior games are not for you." He gave all the young boys a chance. He was not frightened to play you. If you listen nowadays the main argument is that young guys don't get enough games under their belt to progress but that was not the case for us.'

Captain Alex Rae has recently arrived at the club from a spell in English football with Bury. McParland knows he can be the beating heart of the team, the driving force in midfield beside young Ronnie Glavin. St Mirren had wanted his signature but Thistle had beaten them to the pen. He had liked the picture McParland had painted and what he planned for Thistle.

'I met Davie McParland and went through things and I was quite impressed with him although he seemed a wee bit "schoolteacher-like" if you wish,' Rae said.

'That didn't bother me too much. Davie was quite innovative in his style, certainly in his training, and how he wanted the game to be played was unique.

'Previously, you were invariably running up and down the park without a ball whereas in our training the use of a ball and how to work the ball was very important. There was always sufficient time to be on the ball as opposed to running up and down hills. He was a wee bit ahead of his time. Training regimes were very modern.

'Professionally we always got on really well but I kind of believed in speaking up when I had something to say and there were times when I'm sure he wasn't overly happy with what I was having to say, but he probably respected me for making observations that I felt should be made. When we were away on trips, he tended to be almost schoolteacher like in his attempts to keep an eye on us and I can say hand on heart he never had any need to be as strict a disciplinarian as he was.

'He was dealing with a group of guys who were absolutely first-class in their application to their profession as professional footballers.

'But there were times when he was overly strict, although you can't argue with what he achieved in terms of the team he brought together, the youngsters he gave a chance to much earlier than they would have got at another club.

'The refreshing thing was I was only 23 at that time and I was really surprised at the number of younger guys in the squad although there was a couple, Hugh Strachan and Jackie Campbell, who were perhaps a wee bit older. It was a youthful setup so the dynamic of that was a lot of kidology, a lot of capers although when we were training Davie never really let the reins go too much. He was fairly strict. Away from training and football we built a lot of good friendships but Davie ensured training was always down to business.'

* * *

RONNIE GLAVIN is racing to get to training. It is not that he is late, he is just desperate not to miss a minute. His life has been transformed since signing for Thistle and at times he struggles to believe how fortunate he is.

At 16 he had been handed a trial for the national under-18 side. He had been listed as a substitute but when he arrived he was told that the striker who was to be playing was too old and he was being thrown on up front. He scored a hat-trick. By the time he came off the field he was being chased by half a dozen clubs all after his signature. But he had been training at Thistle and chief scout Jimmy Dickie won't countenance him going to anyone else.

His signing is raced through on the Monday morning and, soon after, he is asked to make up the numbers in a game for trialists. It is his first opportunity to grace the Firhill pitch.

'Davie hadn't really seen much of me and I scored five goals in 20 minutes. Then he took me off the field,' said Glavin. 'I wondered what he had done that for and he just looked at me and said, "This isn't your level, son." The next thing I was in the reserves and I scored on my debut. Looking back, he was just saying to me "this isn't for you, you need to go further".'

If that meant training every hour of every day Glavin is fine with that.

'I couldn't wait to get to training. I loved it, I couldn't get enough of it,' he said. 'Davie was helping you to do what you loved doing which was playing football. It was great. At the time in Glasgow all you had to do was play football, all you wanted to do was play football.

'The good thing about Thistle was the opportunity we were given by them. It was a fantastic club – the people, the staff, the fans – I have nothing but good memories of everybody because they gave us the opportunity, taking us out of the back streets and making us into something.

They took ordinary lads and educated them.

'Davie was young, a legend at the club, and they wanted to keep him so he did his coaching and he felt that the way forward was to get younger players. He created a good base for the young guys to come in. I was 16 when I signed and he became a father figure. Everything that he did was based on the boys, looking after the boys; he was educating us in so many ways. It was fantastic.

'I came from Garthamlock and you had nothing, I didn't even have a suit. You were lucky to have clothes and then all of a sudden you've gone there and are getting a pre-match meal and everything. Davie was helping you to do what you loved doing, which was playing football. It was great.

'When you look at the players in the cup final team, most of them were internationals or became internationals. When can you start a youth policy and have six players coming through to your first team who all go on and play for their country? It doesn't happen.

'So, when you have six internationals on the pitch, you have a chance whoever you play. Davie nurtured all these lads and every one of them was a class act.

'The involvement at the club changed you and the success came because we were all willing to work hard with a young manager who was enthusiastic. He was on top of us if anything wasn't right. He just kept everybody on the straight and narrow, every day.

'I owe Davie everything. He was a fabulous man and a great mentor. Make no mistake, whatever happened at that club is all down to one man and that was Davie McParland. No question about it. One hundred per cent.'

* * *

McPARLAND and his backroom staff have constructed the way they want to play. It has been successful in the lower division and they start off the new campaign with the win against Rangers. It convinces them that sticking with it is the best course of action.

His theory is that attack is the best form of defence. Keep the ball in the opposition half for as long as possible. If the play is concentrated there then it stands to reason there is less chance of conceding a goal. It doesn't always work, and the team will suffer some heavy defeats, but there is a freshness to the approach. And it has taken many sides in the First Division by surprise.

'The boys had pace and he used everybody's best attributes,' said defender Jackie Campbell. 'His attitude was, "If you are in their half of the park then they can't score goals." It was all about attacking and getting it up to the front men and letting them do the job as quickly as you could and leave it with them. If they scored three, we would score four, that was just the name of the game. He was all about scoring goals and if you were in their half of the park then they couldn't score.

'But he could also help young boys because Davie was a good player as well. It was an enthusing time at Thistle. Everybody was going well and everybody was running on the top of the grass. You just get that, and that is what makes good football, when you have belief in yourself and you were never defeated until you were defeated. We were always on the way forward, always on the front foot.'

Chief scout Jimmy Dickie has an eye for talent – even if at first glance his targets look unlikely.

'Look at young John Gibson there,' McParland says in an interview with journalist Ken Gallacher. 'When Jimmy Dickie first brought him here he was just a "skelf". I looked at him and then at the scout and Jimmy seemed to read my mind. He just shrugged and said "he can play". I signed him then and he's proved that he can play.'

Winger Denis McQuade is another to benefit from the McParland/Dickie double act.

'He had a wee bit of a soft spot for me because I was not your typical guy that he was dealing with,' he said. 'I could construct an argument and at times he would pull me up on that and say, "I don't care what you're saying, this is what you're doing."

'I found him very fair. I think I was lucky that he had been a winger himself. As were Bobby Lawrie and Johnny Gibson, in that he believed in wing play.

'While I [caused him to tear] his hair out many times, it was only many years later at an event with him that he said the one thing I brought to the party was a bit of unpredictability and that was why he brought me on as sub a lot – just to try and make something happen. He was very understanding. And straight-talking; he didn't suffer fools gladly. I loved working under him. I thought he was tactically very aware and always gave a lot of thought to what he was trying to convey.'

'He just saw things, him and Jimmy between them,' said Ronnie Glavin. 'They hunted all these young players and Davie just nurtured them. He was like an adopted father, or stepfather, make no mistake about that.'

Frank Coulston is in agreement.

'It was a good squad of players no question of that,' he said. 'There was a togetherness about it that is for sure and a lot of skill in the team. You have to credit Davie McParland because it started when he took over as manager and the club weren't in great shape. Davie clearly had a vision for the club which meant not only getting back up from the Second Division to the First Division but building the club up. And he did that pretty shrewdly.

'At the time I wasn't too aware of it because you are too busy playing and I was part-time, teaching and had a young family so life was hectic. But if you think back now to what Davie did it was something else because he brought us back up that very season, which was a difficult task in itself yet, at the same time, he was building the club back up from the depths.

'I hadn't played too much and was never a favourite of Scot Symon. In fact, I thought I'd be released that season but Davie kept me. That gives you a lease of life and a wee bit of confidence – that the manager wants you. He kept that backbone and brought Bobby Gray, Hugh Strachan, Alex Rae, good experienced professionals to add to that group. Alex Rae to my mind was the heart of the team. In midfield he could win the ball cleanly and his range of passing was good so I always rated Alex very highly.

'He added young players Rough, Forsyth, McQuade, Gibson, Lawrie and blended that youth and experience and that helps.

'He was an excellent manager who knew the game well and had been a good player for Thistle, a great servant. He clearly knew where he was going and what he was trying to do. I mean, he wouldn't be everyone's cup of tea and we had our moments with Davie, got on well with him one minute and fell foul of him the next. But that is par for the course for most managers.

'He was thinking ahead [but] I didn't appreciate it at the time. He was Mr Partick Thistle and they should not have let him go. Davie could fall out with folk but you have to realise what you have got. That we've got something here and we should hang on to it.'

* * *

Drive along Strathblane Road in Milngavie heading out of the town on a journey that will take you towards Blanefield and the last road on the left before you head out into the country is Roselea Drive. Head up to where the drive ends in a quiet cul-de-sac and this is where the McParlands have made their home.

Over the fence from their back garden is an open field and beyond that, over the boundary wall and up a steep slope, lies the vast expanse of water that makes up the Craigmaddie and Mugdock reservoirs. Completed at the end of the 19th century, the reservoirs are an engineering masterpiece and hold hundreds of millions of litres of water to supply the city of Glasgow. They are a popular place for walkers, but McParland can often be found pounding round the 5km of pathways keeping himself fit ahead of the start of a new season. The views are spectacular; north to the Campsie Fells, west to the Kilpatrick Hills and, from some of its most exposed vantage points, south over the city of Glasgow itself in splendid panorama. It is the kind of place that offers spectacular vistas whatever the weather, as picturesque in winter as in the height of summer. The kind of place you can watch the weather coming towards you and know what to expect in ten minutes' time.

It is a perfect spot for Davie and wife Terry to bring up their three girls – Yvonne, Tracy and Hazel, each of whom dote on their dad. As a dyed-in-the-wool football man, if he desired a son with whom to talk about the game, he doesn't let it show. Family life to McParland, with his girls, is everything. Their home in Milngavie a domestic bliss.

'Fantastic,' is the word Yvonne uses to describe the kind of man her father was. 'He was a great dad, a great family man. My mum and the three of us meant he was surrounded by women all his days but that was maybe a good thing because if ever there was a man who liked to get spoiled it was my dad, so we all looked after him. And he loved us.

'It was great. Mum would take me to the football from when I was three years old but as a family we all enjoyed the football. Whatever club dad was at we would go and watch the games.'

Was football discussed in the house?

'He tried to explain the offside rule once, with salt and pepper and dishes,' said Yvonne. 'If you are talking tactics absolutely not but latterly my dad and I went to a lot of football so I knew a lot of players he was scouting.'

McParland's extended family is the team he has built at Firhill. Many are fresh-faced kids just starting out on their footballing journey. That puts great responsibility on the manager to guide them, to chastise them when they get it wrong but to allow them leeway, offer understanding, for their tender years. He himself is only 36 years of age. A one-club legend, his move from the dressing room to the manager's office has been seamless yet speedy. It is easy to forget that not so long ago he was still playing.

'He did a lot of his coaching badges when still a player so he was planning ahead [and knew] what he was wanting to do,' said Yvonne. 'My dad took a lot of things in his stride. He was a very modest man but very confident in his own ability. I don't think it would daunt my dad moving into coaching. He played for them, then he was captain and he was coach and then assistant manager, then manager. He came up through the ranks and learned his trade. He was confident in his own abilities and I don't think he would have found that stressful.

'He was only 36 when he won the cup so he was young, really young, but he had an interest in their wellbeing on and off the pitch. He would see himself as a mentor rather than a father figure although a lot of them were teenagers when he took over.'

Mentor? Father figure? Call it what you want. What is not in doubt is the influence McParland has had on his players. That conversation with Robert Reid in the café in Milngavie, when the side was struggling to climb off the floor after relegation, seems a lifetime away now.

History awaits them. This team that McParland built.

'As long as you did what you were told you were fine,' said full-back Alex Forsyth. 'He was a good tactician. He was the first one to bring the likes of myself into the team when I came back from Arsenal when I was only 16 or 17. I came through the reserve teams and broke into the first team. So, he was instrumental in starting my career.

'He was a gentleman.'

CHAPTER 3

THE BAIRNS

'MIGHTY McQUADE THE TWO-GOAL HERO' screams one morning headline while another shouts 'McQUADE SLAMS JAGS INTO THE FINAL'. The newspapers lie scattered on the floor at Firhill. They have already been discussed and digested by the players and staff who have assembled the morning after a wonderful night before. In front of 20,000 fans at Hampden, Davie McParland's side have marched into the League Cup Final after their 2-0 win over a Falkirk side whose overconfidence of reaching the final let down their guards.

Certainly, one member of the Bairns team was sure his side would triumph.

'The prospect of a Hampden semi-final electrified the population of Falkirk, proving how much potential the town and its surrounding district had for supporting a major football club,' wrote Sir Alex Ferguson in his autobiography *Managing my Life*. 'The Thistle, one of my native city's greatest institutions, would be interesting opponents. They had a popularity that did not rely on achievement. For decades they had been a favourite target of every comedian working the Glasgow theatres, but their loyal fans regarded them with loving indulgence, gladly tolerating rapid fluctuations of form that took them from the scintillating to the abysmal

' Ideally, the club should have had joint chairmen – Dr Jekyll and Mr Hyde. They had earned any number of nicknames, some straightforward, others mockingly fanciful: the Jags, the Harry Wraggs, the Maryhill Magyars, the Partick Hungarians.

'At their best they might have given Puskás and his 1950s Hungarians a fright, but at their worst a team picked from drunks leaving the pub at closing time might have beaten them. To support them or play for them was to be on an emotional rollercoaster.

'I was confident Falkirk could handle the Thistle, as I had been able over the years to score plenty of goals against them. So much for assumptions. At Hampden on the big night, Thistle were in their Magyar mood and their two wingers Lawrie and McQuade tore us to ribbons.'

Confirmation of who Thistle face in the final will not be determined until Celtic play St Mirren the following evening but everyone knows it will be Jock Stein's side. Few can touch them.

Still, the players who are at the ground are in buoyant mood and McQuade's checked trousers are a bit of a giveaway that football is not on their minds. The manager has given them a day off and 18 holes at Hayston Golf Club just outside Kirkintilloch beckon. But that is not before more media duties. Thistle are hot to trot now and journalists and photographers are never far away from Firhill.

It is why, on the morning of 5 October 1971, McQuade is being pictured incongruously out on the Firhill pitch, posing at the finish of his follow-through with Alan Rough, John Hansen and Bobby Lawrie looking on, leaning on their golf bags.

'No manager could have had a better response from his team,' Davie McParland says. 'The boys all did well. They pulled that extra bit out and we are so pleased we are in the final.

'Denis McQuade certainly paid his way with the goals.

'Now we are only 90 minutes away from the League Cup which is something I didn't really expect at the outset to the season.'

Nobody could argue that Thistle do not deserve their place in the final because theirs has been the longest of journeys. Arbroath, East Fife and Raith have all been conquered home and away during the group stage. Alloa were sent packing in a supplementary round required because of the odd number of teams.

And then there was St Johnstone in the quarter-final.

Thistle trailed 2-0 from the first leg at Muirton Park. McParland had tinkered with his tactics and lived to regret it. On his journey home from Perth, Robert Reid had all but conceded the tie.

'I was resigned to the fact that our League Cup aspirations were in tatters yet again just as they had been in all the previous years I had supported Thistle,' he wrote in his book *Red and Yellow Forever*. 'My travelling companions on the 60-mile trip home were regaled with my customary optimism. "Well, that's that … 2-0 it's far too big a deficit to make up … if they score again it's all over!"

'I have always been prepared to look on the bright side in football. It's just that only on rare occasions have I been able to find it.'

As it turns out, this time Reid has little reason for pessimism. Back in front of a packed Firhill for the return leg, Thistle go goal-crazy in a 5-1 triumph.

Jimmy Bone and Frank Coulston scored doubles, Johnny Gibson a single.

'At half-time at Firhill I saw a couple of people had taken ill,' said Alex Forsyth. 'One or two old ones died because they couldn't believe we were doing so well.'

'The magnificent, tireless men of Partick Thistle crashed their way into the League Cup semi-final in glorious style at near hysterical Firhill,' wrote journalist James Sanderson. 'This was surely one of the finest hours in the 95-year history of the club.

'This Thistle performance was essentially a triumph of teamwork and enthusiasm, pace and courage.

All this allied to a never-say-die spirit.'

'We had to come back against St Johnstone after getting beat 2-0 but we just knew we were going to win,' said Jackie Campbell. 'There was a confidence in the team at that time. It was surprising to get beat 2-0 so you just rolled your sleeves up and you came back and got on with it. I mean, we scored five that night.'

That glorious night at Firhill set up the semi-final prospect of Falkirk at the national stadium – just one match, one more hurdle, before a Hampden final. And ahead of the game everyone in the team is buzzing.

Apart from one.

* * *

JOHNNY GIBSON is everything you want in a Thistle player. The winger is fast, skilful, and strong on the ball despite being short in stature. He's also a bit of a movie star. He wears his hair long, is a follower of fashion and the leader of trends within the Firhill dressing room. If he wasn't in the first team he'd be in a band.

He lit up the season in Thistle's first game back in the top flight. If Rangers and their fans didn't know who he was then they most certainly did after he ripped them to shreds in only 45 minutes on the opening day of the league campaign with two goals and an assist, and all that before injury curtailed his involvement at half-time.

'Displaying amazing calmness and composure Gibson ran the legs off the Rangers defence,' wrote Malcolm Munro in the *Evening Times*. 'And when he was running he didn't forget the ball as so many players do. He carried it swiftly and accurately into the opposition defence.'

Perhaps he is reflecting on those good times as he sits with the rest of the team taking their pre-match meal ahead of the semi-final. For Gibson has a problem. An ankle knock has been bothering him since the 2-2 draw with Kilmarnock in the league just days before.

In his mind, Davie McParland has Gibson down as a starter for the game. He knows his skills could be crucial. But he is also aware his talented little winger is struggling and takes him aside, away from the rest of the team.

'How's that knock you've got wee man?' he asks.

The decision is down to the player. Gibson knows it. His mind is racked with dilemma. Only he knows the truth. What he doesn't know is that what he says next is a defining moment in his career.

'I just don't feel it's right, you know?' Gibson said.

'Okay then,' says McParland. 'If it's not right it is pointless putting you in the team.'

'That's fine,' replies Gibson.

Mentally, the manager is now shuffling his pack. Denis McQuade will start on the wing, Tommy Rae comes on to the bench as the one and only substitute.

Mentally, Gibson is wondering if he has done the right thing.

'If I had my time to do over, I would never do that again, say that I'm injured and then not start the match,' said Gibson. 'I could have played and just taken the bonus and got on for maybe 20 minutes but I was thinking more for the team.

'Tommy Rae got the sub spot and Denis scored two goals and kept his place which is fair enough. He gets the place in the final team which was a wee bit disappointing I must say.

'It was a £300 bonus and when we got our wages after the semi-final and I looked in mine I thought, "Where the hell is the money?" I chapped Davie's door and said, "What is the story boss, with the money?"

'He says, "Well, you weren't playing were you? You weren't in the 12". I said "no" and he said, "Well, you're not getting the bonus."

'So, I wouldn't do that again.'

The spotlight then is about to fall on a tall, gangly figure singularly unaware of what fate has in store for him. While one man's misfortune can be another's golden opportunity, it is nothing if that individual does not grab it with both hands or, in McQuade's case, feet.

* * *

DENIS McQUADE had been a regular starter in the Thistle side so the fact that he is to play a supporting role against Falkirk is a surprise. But it is horses for courses as far as McParland is concerned and Gibson is the preferred choice given he is the man in form. McQuade knows it.

He is a polar opposite to Gibson. Where the latter is small, McQuade is tall for a winger. Where Gibson plays with the ball glued to his feet, McQuade gives every appearance that even he doesn't know what he is going to do next. But just as Gibson is a fans' favourite, so too is McQuade.

Both are popular in the dressing room too. Where Gibson is the leader of fashion, McQuade is an esoteric, enigmatic, sometimes perplexing voice.

He is a student at the University of Glasgow but, until the age of 18, had trained for the priesthood and was looking towards Rome and a degree in theology.

He is nicknamed the Mad Monk, or Crazy Horse. Or his own personal favourite, The Madness.

He is one of the first at the club to cultivate a moustache, not popular with manager McParland.

'We all have our idiosyncrasies, boss,' McQuade said after refusing to shave it off. 'I'll gie you effing idio-whatever-they're-called,' McParland had replied.

'I think I'm a better player now in people's memories than I ever was at the time,' he recalled in an interview with *The Scotsman* long after his career was over. 'Don't get me wrong, that's lovely, but I reckon it's less to do with me and more about the nostalgia that's around for my time in the game and the affection that's always been there for Partick Thistle.

'What is the personality of a football club? How do you define it? I don't know, but from the moment I joined Thistle I was aware of the mystique. And the side I played for was a bit different, adventurous, worth the admission money. It would be nice if more teams were like that these days.'

As the time ticks down towards kick-off, McQuade is unaware his plans for the evening are about to change.

'The team had been picked for the Wednesday night for Falkirk and Gibby had been the man in form the previous week,' McQuade said. 'He had started against Kilmarnock and right up until half an hour before kick-off Gibby was going to be playing along with Bobby Lawrie on the other wing.

'But Gibby had said to Jackie Husband and McParland that he didn't think he could play so McParland just turned round and said, "Denis, get stripped, you're playing."'

Thistle start the game nervously as if perhaps spooked by their surroundings.

'We were nervous that night so close [to the final] but so far, that is when the nerves start to set in,' said Jackie Campbell.

But soon they settle into their rhythm. Ronnie Glavin is immense in the middle of the park. Harrowing, grafting, never missing a chance to burst through when a gap appears. Alex Rae is at his best also.

When the first goal arrives on 31 minutes the only surprise is that it has taken so long. Jimmy Bone puts his first chance against the post and then sends the rebound back across the line where McQuade is loitering with intent and hammers home.

The Bairns have their chances. This is a nerve-tingling cup tie until the 87th minute when Falkirk's John Markie is short with a pass back and McQuade pounces once again.

'I got the chance and scored the two goals,' he said. 'The first one was a stramash and the ball presented itself three yards out and even I couldn't miss it. Then, late in the second half, I predicted this guy would pass it back to the goalie and I nipped in and lobbed the keeper.

'I think McParland felt he couldn't very well drop me for the final after I helped to get them there.'

'IT'S SIZZLE' roars one headline the next day as Davie McParland is asked for his reaction to his side's Hampden heroics.

'Teamwork – and sheer hard work took us through,' he says.

As he bids his boys off to the golf course and some well-earned downtime, McParland heads back to his office. He has a cup final to plan for and, after tasting defeat as a player, he has no intention of dining at disappointment's table as a manager – no matter who the opposition are.

Perhaps, however, that can wait. The manager ponders before deciding he'll join his troops on the fairways. All for one and one for all!

CHAPTER 4

THE TEAM – AND SCOTLAND

TOMMY DOCHERTY is assistant manager at Hull City, helping former Arsenal team-mate Terry Neill, when he is approached by journalist Ken Gallacher who asked if he can pass Docherty's number to Scottish Football Association chairman Hugh Nelson. Scotland are without a manager since the departure of Bobby Brown and Docherty has led a fans' poll as the man they want in the international hotseat.

'It's very nice to see the fans still have faith in me,' he says. 'But it doesn't mean very much.'

Perhaps, however, the Tartan Army know something Docherty does not. Because within a matter of hours of Hull losing at Bristol City he is in a meeting with SFA representatives and being offered the international manager's post on a three-game trial basis. Euro qualifiers against Portugal and Belgium then a friendly with Holland – and we'll see what happens after that is the gist of the conversation.

Docherty, of course, accepts. It is why he is standing with the assembled Scotland squad in their windswept Largs training base. Ironically the forthcoming opposition is a team he knows well after a recent spell in charge of Porto. Three of the squad were his former players. He knows how the Portuguese will play but he needs to get that over to his players. It is his first experience with many of them – and he has called on an old friend to help.

Davie McParland has just one more game before the League Cup Final, the visit of St Johnstone to Firhill, but when he takes a call from Docherty asking if he can send a Thistle side down for a bounce game he is keen to come to his nation's, and his pal's, aid. The trip to Largs will provide an interesting alternative to the normal training, no matter how innovative the Thistle manager is in his techniques.

'Partick Thistle have the most promising bunch of young players in the country,' Docherty says. 'The big problem is keeping them together but they could be challenging for league honours very soon.

'They have a talented and good manager in Davie McParland. He is young enough to go out with them in training and the likes and that is what it's all about.

'They have a great quality to compete, and compete well, on the field. In fact, they remind me of the youngsters in the young side I had at Chelsea, a great bunch of lads.

'I have seen Thistle more times this season than any other team – and all away games at that – and they have shown up well.'

McParland scans the players Docherty has selected. Bobby Clark, Sandy Jardine, David Hay, Billy Bremner, Willie Young, Pat Stanton, Jimmy Johnstone, George Graham, John O'Hare, Alex Cropley, Archie Gemmill. The line-up reads like the very cream of Scottish talent from north and south of the border. There are instructions that the game is to be played somewhere below full contact but both managers know that all bets are off when the whistle blows. Anything can happen.

'Tommy Docherty was the Scotland manager and he was a very good friend of Davie McParland,' said Alex Rae. 'I remember playing in it, [and] big Alan [Rough] after we played just quietly said to me, "Wee Billy Bremner was quite impressed with you today, Alex," and I was over the moon. So maybe I remember that because it was one of the few times anybody said that about me.

'I remember playing in the game and playing quite well but it wasn't a 100 per cent game if you know what I mean. There were no flying tackles or anything like that.

'I found it really easy. The reason I found it easy was probably because it was not an important game, just a run-out. But the good players allow you to play, they will not be diving into you when there is no chance of getting the ball.

'I remember enjoying the game and being surprised how easy it was to slot in against these kind of players.

'I never had any concern about injury – you would go out and play each game as it comes. I know the cup final had more importance but the bottom line is if you go into a game thinking what if this or that happens then you wouldn't play at all. I don't, and didn't, have that kind of attitude.'

The game is played at a level below 100 per cent nonetheless.

One scribe watching wrote, 'All 16 players were used for at least a half of the game against Partick whose eager players adopted a pattern likely to be used by the Portuguese. Docherty's presence was all-powerful during the game as he controlled his men from various stances on the touchline. He shouted encouragement and bellowed instructions when needed.'

In the end it finishes 1-1. Both managers are content with what's been achieved and learnt from the run out. Docherty has learnt even more than he would let on. In his notebook he scribbles down some names.

'Forsyth – a fast and attack-minded full-back. I like him.'

'Glavin – has plenty of promise.'

'Rough – a fine prospect, there is no doubt about that.

He is a great kicker of the ball and very safe.'

'Hansen – A ball player and very cool with it. There is no panic from John. He knows what to do with the ball.'

'McQuade – Alert and skilful and also hits a very hard ball'

'The score was of no account at all,' says McParland. 'What Tommy Docherty wanted from Partick Thistle was a chance to try out various partnerships and to see how the players performed against strong opposition.

'As far as Partick Thistle were concerned we learnt a great deal in going down to Largs. It was most heartening to see how the Scots lads worked.'

Scotland would go on to beat Portugal 2-1 with goals from John O'Hare and Archie Gemmill in front of nearly 59,000 at Hampden just 48 hours later. Perhaps, in some little way, Thistle can claim some of the credit.

* * *

DAVIE McPARLAND is in his office at Firhill and surrounded by his inner circle. There is Scot Symon, Jackie Husband and physio Willie Ross. There have been two league games since the semi-final win over Falkirk and one curious call to national service, and the Thistle boss has much on his mind.

An away draw at Dunfermline and a home win over St Johnstone have maintained the feel-good around Firhill. McParland has concentrated on keeping everything as normal as is possible. He could have taken the team away for a few days but past experience has taught him that time out of the limelight is not always a good thing. Twice as a player at Thistle he went away before the League Cup Final, and twice he was on the losing side.Better he feels to have kept everything as usual, as close to the norm as possible. The full-time players can train as normal, the part-timers in on a Tuesday and Thursday. And all can continue with the home comforts. Nothing different. It is only the all-conquering Celtic, in a Hampden final. What is there to be scared of?

The games against Dunfermline and St Johnstone have offered further insight into the character of his team. At East End Park they showed their courage to come from behind twice for a well-deserved point. At home to St Johnstone, Thistle had dominated from the off, lost a careless goal and then scored twice in two minutes to secure the points. The fans that day were in buoyant mood, eagerly anticipating their trip to Hampden and knowing that their team is in good form.

There are concerns for McParland, however. He looks towards Willie Ross as the discussion turns to matters from the treatment room. Ronnie Glavin missed the win over St Johnstone with an ankle knock that is causing real concern while Ross has also been giving attention to captain Alex Rae, Bobby Lawrie and Alex Forsyth.

Ross is the kind of worker ant every club needs. He is a gem and a gentleman, a confidante of the players and a sounding board for the manager. He keeps feet on the ground and heads out of the clouds and he has had his work cut out since the semi-final win to keep minds focused.

Ross has good news. Rae, Lawrie and Forsyth should all be fine and are causing no worries. Glavin, the industrious midfielder, is a different matter. He might not make it; it is touch and go.

McParland ponders for a second. Really this shouldn't be a problem. Ever since he took charge at the club after the relegation to the Second Division he has called upon the same cohort of players, ignoring those who perhaps fear they are too young for such responsibility. But he kept the faith and trusted them to get the club back to the top division. He trusted in their youth, their lack of inhibitions, their lack of fear. He knows he has work to do to strengthen the squad but the key elements he can count on. Not bad for a side that cost the dizzying sum of £250 – and all that spent on bringing Denis McQuade from St Rochs.

'The boys learned a lot of their trade in the Second Division,' McParland says. 'The talent was always there but the season we went down they had neither the confidence nor the experience necessary for the First Division.

'When we were relegated it seemed tragic for the club. But it helped us in the end.

The boys gained confidence in their own ability in the Second Division. Before we were relegated the ball was like a hot potato. The lads had been frightened to try anything. The pressure on them was too much. In the Second Division they re-found themselves and by the end of the season I knew we would make our mark in the First Division.

'I like to think of us as a unit. If a player is injured then I can have someone ready to do his particular job.'

Injury aside, he reasons, this team picks itself yet there are decisions to make. He knows that by sticking to his formation that has served him so well, so far, he runs the risk of being outnumbered in midfield. It puts a great deal of the onus on Alex Rae and Ronnie Glavin. It is why he is so anxious Glavin must play.

He also must decide on the conundrum of the wide men. John Gibson had been in sparkling form until injury saw him miss out against Falkirk. Denis McQuade stepped up and grabbed his chance, scoring both goals. That should have cemented his place in the starting line-up but McParland has another reason to start the gangly winger – a special plan for nullifying Bobby Murdoch.

He has told the press that, until he sees how the injured players fare, he cannot pick a definite team for Hampden. But now, in the sanctuary of his office, it is time to do just that.

He takes his pen and lifts a blank sheet of paper. On it he writes the number '1'.

Alan Rough has played all but one game so far this season. He will go on to play every one until the end of the campaign. The only game he has missed has been the 5-0 home win over Raith in the group stages of the League Cup. Coincidentally that would be the only game captain Alex Rae misses as well over the entire season.

'He's courageous,' says McParland of the 19-year-old. 'He has a good pair of hands and collects crossfield balls with ease.

'Actually, if anything, we take his talent too much for granted.'

Rough's emergence as Scotland's next great goalkeeping hope is all the more remarkable given the childhood accident that so nearly ended in catastrophe.

Rough was just ten years of age when, out playing with pals, he slipped on a fallen door that helped them reach a hidden football pitch and crashed into the sharp hinges that had gone unnoticed previously.

'I remember the searing jolt of agony as it ripped through my arm,' Rough recalls in his autobiography *The Rough and The Smooth*. 'I was screaming and yelling out "help me for God's sake, it hurts like hell". And then when I glanced down, I saw the flesh that had been pierced clean through to the bone.'

Rushed to hospital, the medical prognosis was not good. A first doctor concluded that there was little that could be done to save the arm.

'I was ten years old,' says Rough. 'Numb with worry, already shocked and scared, and here I was being told that all my football dreams were being dashed even before they had really begun.'

A second doctor, however, held an alternative view and was confident that with speedy surgery the arm could be saved.

'Despite my never discovering the name of that doctor who saved me, he commands my undying gratitude,' Rough says.

Nine months recovery were required to get back to full fitness but the scar remains.

'It's still there,' he told journalist Hugh MacDonald in an interview with the *Daily Mail*. 'You could see the bone, like a bone a dog eats! I always say I was lucky.'

Perhaps it was that run-in with disaster that shapes Rough's easy-going outlook on life now. Since breaking into the team he has been a fixture. And despite the pressure of being the last line of defence at such a young age, Rough is unfazed by the responsibility.

'Almost immediately after I arrived Rough got the number one shirt and for a young boy he just didn't worry about anything, he was so relaxed, which did him well for his future football career,' said Alex Rae. 'He was just so laid back. A smashing big goalkeeper and clearly destined for better things.

'He was strong at everything and I don't say that lightly. He didn't have a weakness. He was actually a good football player as well. He used to star in the wee bounce games, he had a smashing left foot. As a goalkeeper he had all that was required, his temperament was superb.'

What's more important for the young keeper is the trust his team-mates have in him despite his tender years.

'It is absolute,' said Alex. 'If you have a goalkeeper who has obvious failings you are almost having to do his job in and around the box. You are maybe going to attempt to header shots or [deal with a] situation. You didn't need to do that with big Alan. He was the boss in the box and that was it.'

At number two,

John Hansen is a powerful, penetrating threat down the right who has found favour ahead of the reliable Ian Reid. But Hansen has the engine and attacking instincts that make him perfect for McParland's forward-thinking style, even if it left the centre-halves exposed.

THE TEAM – AND SCOTLAND

'They used to shout at us to come back but Alex Forsyth and I just kept going,' Hansen said.

'That was just the way the team played. That was McParland's way. The full-backs just attacked all the time, I mean we didn't know any better. We just attacked and attacked.

'Sometimes we'd win 4-0 or 5-0 and sometimes we'd get beat by that.

'People say to me there was no fear but that was just the way McParland had it drummed into us for months before, that this was how we were going to play and attack and sometimes we'll win, sometimes we won't.

'There was a really good mix. The older players would try and calm the younger players down because if McParland told us to attack that was it, it could be 1-0 with 30 seconds to go and other teams would be protecting that, whereas we would be bombing up the park to try and get two. Hugh and Jackie would be shouting us back and calming us down.'

'Big John was a no-thrills, athletic, good football player,' said Alex Rae. 'Not a tippy-tappy, he would get the ball, he was very straightforward. He would get forward – we had two really aggressive attacking full-backs in John and Alex Forsyth.

'John didn't get forward just as much as Alex did but [he] was a real reliable big individual.'

Wearing three,

Alex Forsyth is a similar threat to Hansen on the left but also has the talent to ping a ball to a striker's feet from 50 yards. He provides an outlet and an attacking option. Thistle, at the time under Scot Symon, snapped up the young defender from Arsenal and had watched him flourish in the team. And what energy he has. McParland knows Forsyth will run all day up. He has also formed a potent partnership with winger Bobby Lawrie and McParland is well aware how important this double act will be.

'I played left-back more than he did,' Alex Rae laughed when asked about Forsyth. 'He had only one route, as soon as he got the ball he was away and it was common sense I would slot into his role at left-back.

37

'Alex on the left-hand side gave you a goal threat as well as a good attacking option. What he used to do at training, before we even kicked a ball, he would run on to the park at Firhill or wherever we trained and he would just blooter the ball. Now, in modern-day football, physiotherapists and sports scientists would be absolutely aghast at what he used to do. He would just run on to the park, a wee jog, and then he would just blooter the ball, and he could hit a ball too!'

McParland knows the importance of the midfield area to the outcome of Saturday's final. It is why he is so anxious over the condition of Ronnie Glavin's ankle. He's confident it will hold up. Glavin is the type of determined character who will play through the pain barrier anyway. Thistle will need his grit and determination but also the attacking thrusts through gaps in the middle of the park. The Thistle boss has no fear writing down Glavin's name for the number four shirt but he intends to include the reliable Charlie Smith in his plans right up to the last minute.

'He was quite simply, in my entire football career, one of the best players I ever played with or against,' said Alex Rae. 'Ronnie was two-footed, he was fast, he was mobile, he was even a good goalkeeper. He was an all-round football player. He had good ball control, could beat men, could make passes, you name it, he could do it. That sounds a wee bit simple but he could tackle, he was good in the air, had an absolutely phenomenal shot.

'I really couldn't give him more praise. I can't think of anything he couldn't do. And he was good at all the basic stuff as well.'

The number five shirt is a no-brainer. McParland is on record as saying moving Jackie Campbell from full-back to centre-half has been one of the best decisions of his fledgling managerial career. Campbell has been outstanding and has the vital experience this young Thistle side needs. If only his early career had not been so blighted by injury, and if he had turned full-time, who knows how far Campbell could have gone?

'See if he didn't have a good job away from football, I would have been very surprised if Jackie wouldn't have got into a Scotland team at some point,' said Alex Rae. 'He kept everything very simple. He always tried to play a pass; very seldom would you see Jackie giving it the howf. His timing and positional sense was superb. Initially he wasn't in the team and eventually he got in and, well, he was never out the team after that.

'Jackie had been there a long time before I arrived. He was the perfect professional. A boy who just lived a good life and didn't misbehave. He was never under pressure. Playing against the best kind of players he was just outstanding.

'Underrated? That would be absolutely true.'

This cup run has been a fairytale for Hugh Strachan, the father figure of the team and wearing number six. Now also assisting in a coaching capacity, he would have thought his career in the first team was at an end. That was until McParland got the manager's role and recognised, when looking for another experienced anchor at the back, that the answer was right on his doorstep. Strachan's partnership with Jackie Campbell is also a huge part of the Thistle success story, as is the pair's ability to guide the youngsters around them.

'Hughie was a good guy first of all. He was respected,' said Alex Rae. 'The one good thing about Hughie was he was totally dependable. Hughie would never try anything risky. He had good positional sense, good in the air, good in the tackle. No thrills. You would never see Hughie trying to give it the Jim Baxter stuff in the 18-yard box. But he was just so dependable.

'With his additional role as a coach he took lots of the training sessions and in all the time he was doing that [he took] the warm-ups, we used to give him stick, because our warm-ups were long. You were never going to get any pulled muscles when Hughie was in charge of the training. I can't remember anybody having injuries during the course of Hughie's time as a coach. The warm-ups might last half an hour but we all benefitted through his treatment of us.'

McParland's pen hangs in the air and for a second or two he ponders his number seven. Then he writes the name of Denis McQuade. Talented, fast, strong, unpredictable. He deserves his place in the starting line-up after his semi-final heroics. But McParland has another reason to pick McQuade. He wants him to get into Bobby Murdoch's face; whenever the Celtic man is on the ball, McParland wants McQuade snapping at his heels. It is another reason to plump for McQuade ahead of the unfortunate Jimmy Gibson.

'Big Denis, he played on the right wing in the final but he also played on the left wing too, and me sort of playing on the left-hand side of the park you just didn't know what was going to do,' said Alex Rae. 'There were times when you would expect a pass from him and you wouldn't get it and there were other times when he was running away from you and he would back heel it to you. He really kept you on your toes. An old-fashioned football player if ever there was one.

'He was quick, he was good with the ball at his feet, he had a really powerful shot and he scored quite a lot of goals. He was the unknown quantity and opposition teams just didn't know how to handle him. I don't know if Denis knew what he would do next.

'He could play left, right or through the middle. I was never the quickest and I used to envy the boys who could run as quick as that, Bobby, Denis, Ronnie Glavin, all flying machines.'

At number eight,

Frank Coulston is the perfect team man, hard-working, able to bring the best out in others around him. His partnership with Jimmy Bone is one of the key components of the team. He looked as if he was on the way out of the club until the manager intervened and persuaded him to stay. What a decision that has proven to be.

This double act was to be a key part of the McParland battle plan. If the wide men can stretch the game by tearing up the flanks, then Bone and Coulston can give Celtic palpitations by exploiting the empty spaces on the vast Hampden pitch. They can give the Celtic defence real problems.

The key is not to restrict their movement. For months he has been working on a move that in essence was incredibly simple, allowing both front men to swap, but the players had found it difficult to implement. McParland knew his players were frustrated with the constant work on the training ground to get it right. But he stuck it out until it clicked. He is confident the Celtic defence won't be able to cope with the movement of his frontmen combined with the attacking forays of his wingers.

It may look like a 4-4-2 formation but in essence it is 4-2-4.

'The week before the final Davie worked on Frank and myself going and doing our runs,' said Jimmy Bone. 'Everybody used to say we were telepathic and that the two of us knew each other's game but what people didn't realise was that we worked a bit on developing it. We were a wee bit fortunate because the two of us were fairly pacy.

'But Davie planted a seed in the two of our heads. "You two will give them problems, big empty spaces at Hampden. Make sure you make these runs," he told us. He kind of brainwashed into it a wee bit Davie.'

'It was good to play with Jimmy,' said Frank Coulston. 'He always says I was good for him but he was good for me and we dovetailed well. He was a willing worker, a willing runner. He worked hard at his game and became an excellent player, taking the ball and linking the play up front.

'Davie's message was don't change anything for anybody. He would never say to Jimmy or myself come back and do a wee bit more defending – we were always thinking of going forward and so were the wide guys, Denis and Bobby Lawrie. The wide guys went up and down and that left Jimmy and me to cover the width of the pitch really but we were fit. Davie kept us fit, you certainly knew you had been in a training session with Davie.'

'I first played against Frank when I was with East Fife reserves, I was maybe 18 and he was playing for Jordanhill teacher training college,' said Alex Rae. 'The first time we played against him I couldn't believe the pace of this boy. He just was outstanding, good control, left and right foot, quick. I can't remember the score but I'm sure he scored a couple.

'But from that time forward you almost accidentally kept track of how he was doing and when I joined up at Firhill it was really great to be reacquainted with him. An absolutely superb individual as a person but also as a football player. His mobility and pace. Him and Jimmy Bone, I would never have liked to play against those two because you would end up just having to kick them. If they were that quick you need to deal with them.

'He brought a maturity into the team, a kind of calmness, that when you were under the cosh, not doing well, the likes of Hugh, Frank, Jackie, their experience just shone through and it helped a lot in a lot of situations.'

McParland hardly pauses as he writes the name of Jimmy Bone on the sheet of paper for number nine. Hard as nails, quick and lethal in front of goal with boot or head, Bone had been full-time but had reverted back to part-time football after the club gave him permission to resume his training as an electrician in the coal mines. The manager liked that work ethic – and the way he and Coulston had worked to become the perfect striking double act. It was almost as if there was a telepathy between the pair, both knowing when to split, when to make opposite runs to present greater options for the midfielders to find a pass.

'He could run like a stallion,' said Alex Rae. 'I'm surprised he didn't burst a few balls the way he kicked them. He had good pace and an eye for the goal. I would be very surprised if he wasn't our leading goalscorer during the time he was there.

'He was built like a brick shithouse. Raw, his touch wasn't great all the time, but as his career progressed his touch never let him down and the career he had tells you what a superb player he was with the amount of games he played.

'He had a superb partnership with Coulston. It was the brainchild of Davie McParland. There was this thing, when Ronnie and I had the ball they would make a cross over run and you knew either to fire it over one side or the other. The amount of goals we got just through that simple wee routine was quite surprising. He must have been a nightmare to play against because if somebody can run quicker than you then there is not an awful lot you can do.'

What a captain Alex Rae has proved to be since his arrival from Bury last season. McParland had to work hard to persuade him to come to Firhill and reject an approach from St Mirren. They didn't see eye-to-eye all the time. The number ten would often speak up, offer a contrary opinion, but, in his heart, McParland welcomed that.

McParland had laughed when he read a recent interview with Rae which quoted an unnamed team-mate, 'When we go out on the field it's not the opposition we fear about – it's Alex.'

But the interview also gave an insight into the psyche of his skipper.

'I believe it is part of my job to urge the lads on,' he says. 'Some players need to be prodded a bit to give their best. I like to think that I keep them on their toes.

'It also helps my own game. It doesn't do me any harm to let off steam. And it increases my commitment to every match.'

Rae and Glavin are going to be key in this final. They must drive forward, be the beating heart of the team, but also cover and make up for the fact that they will be one less in the middle of the park.

McParland has total faith in them both.

'Alex was a great midfield player,' said Ronnie Glavin. 'In today's game Alex would have more of a holding role. He was experienced, did the sensible thing, played the right ball and was tough and hard. He was an excellent, first-class player. You kind of concede space if you only have two in there like that which we found out to our detriment later on in games, at times in Europe teams play an extra man in there and it was too much for us.'

'But Alex was tops. Look, we had a really good balance through the team.'

McParland allows himself a little smile as he writes down Bobby Lawrie's name by number 11. This unassuming little winger has pace to burn and is comfortable on either flank. In fact, McParland will encourage both him and McQuade to switch if the need arises. Lawrie is the type of winger all fans love. He runs at defenders, twisting and turning. If width is to be key at Hampden, then so too will Lawrie.

'Wee Bobby was virtually wide left just about all the time I played, I think,' said Alex Rae. 'He was just so quick and he had a wee routine that got him by defenders and the only thing they could do to stop him was reverting to violence. He would score goals, pull you out a hole if you were toiling, but his pace was his biggest attribute and his ability to get the ball on target.

'For a thin sort of boy, he was a strong boy. Hugh Strachan was a brickie in his early days and they used to have the odd arm wrestle and none of the two of them would ever win, they would have been there yet. Wee Bobby was undefeated at the arm wrestling with anybody else. A strong wee man.'

The manager has a heavy heart when he writes the final name of his squad on his bit of paper. If only he could get 12 men in his starting line-up. John Gibson has been in fine form, and is a quality player. There are many who would argue he should start. Yet just because he is on the bench does not mean he is not integral to the plan. Far from it. If Thistle find themselves in need of a potent force who better to bring on? And if they find themselves in front with the clock ticking down, well, get Gibson on the park. Get him to slow it down, keep the ball, take it for a walk. In the entire squad there is nobody better suited to the task.

'Wee John was a complicated wee man,' said Alex Rae. 'We were quite pally. He was a real wee character, a real sharp wee dresser and he also had a wee sports car. He was the man. He used to get a lot of stick and occasionally he would take the bait. Inconsistent would be the word but if he could only have maintained a proper level, well, he wouldn't have been playing for Partick Thistle to be honest with you.

'One of his outstanding games when we got promoted was against Rangers; he tore them apart. On his day he was outstanding, a similar type of player to Willie Henderson or Jimmy Johnstone. He had pace and trickery and the very fact that I am comparing him with who I just mentioned, well, it really says it all.'

McParland raises his head and looks at those trusted lieutenants around the room. There are no dissenting voices. To the 12 names he adds two others. Tommy Rae and Charlie Smith had significant claims for a place in the 11. They are both trusted and reliable fixtures in the squad but not everyone can play. Others, such as Andy Anderson, the legendary Donnie McKinnon, Nobby Clark and Ian Reid, have all played a part on the road to Hampden. Sadly, they will have only a watching brief on the day.

Rough, Hansen, Forsyth, Glavin, Campbell, Strachan, McQuade, Bone, Coulston, Rae, Lawrie. Sub: Gibson.

If each man in that selection meeting that day was honest, they would admit it was not the toughest of choices.

And as Alex Rae confirmed, 'We knew the team maybe a couple of days before the final but it almost picked itself. Wee Gibby playing or not – that was the only decision that might have been debatable.'

McParland sits back. There is little more he can do now. He has kept the build-up to the final as simple as possible. He hasn't changed much, hasn't filled his players' heads with tactical instructions or changes to the norm. He hasn't complicated matters but has worked hard to ensure the week has been as ordinary as possible. What a journey this has been, and one not devoid of speed bumps. It has been 18 months in the making but at times it feels like a decade.

Those who questioned his determination to stick with his young guns have had their fears allayed. The crowds are flocking back to Firhill now to come and see this team, his team.

Thistle are no joke any more but he is happy that most commentators are not giving his side a chance. Because he knows they can play a bit.

And he has a feeling – a very funny feeling.

CHAPTER 5

THE MORNING

THE night shift at Polmaise pit had not long clocked off and Jimmy Bone was awakening from a night of fitful sleep, tossing and turning as the dark hours headed toward the dawn light. He had hoped for a lie-in but there was little chance of that. Perhaps the nerves were beginning already, tingling in his stomach.

As point of fact, Bone should have been working that shift too, returning to his in-laws' Fallin home near Stirling as the darkness of the October morning lifted. But the powers-that-be had deemed that such a possibility was not the best use of the 22-year-old's time or talents. Not when he had a cup final to prepare for against a Celtic side standing head and shoulders above any in the land and marshalled by a managerial colossus in Jock Stein. Bone would need all the help he could get and his employers and colleagues ensured they were doing their bit. There was camaraderie in coal. What was it Stein said about the solidarity of miners? 'You might not know the guy beside you but he could save your life.' In such an unforgiving environment people pulled together.

He had been working night shifts all that week anyway, juggling spells in the subterranean darkness at Polmaise with Tuesday and Thursday trips to train with Partick Thistle.

'I worked down the pits on the Thursday prior to the final,' he said. 'But the boys looked after me. They made sure I didn't do too much.

'I finished at 6.30 on the Friday morning. I was supposed to go in again on the Friday but they said stay away. That was out of the question.

'A lot of my family worked there. I'm from a big family so a lot of my uncles worked there.

'I was an apprentice electrician. I'd gone full-time [in football] and I realised that was stupid – I had only something like around a year to do in order to be qualified so I went back. The club were very good about it.

'I was trying to take a long lie-in but not managing it. I was up bright and early. I was just very, very excited.'

Fallin was one of those small towns that revolved around its pits. Although long gone now, this main source of employment for the village meant everybody knew everybody else.

As Bone left that morning, the fact that there was no ceremonial crowd to cheer him off and only a few well-wishers to wish him luck should not be taken as a sign that nobody cared. If you were to think that you would be wrong. Club allegiances were being put to one side and, for one day only, Fallin had a 'Thistle Supporters' Association'.

'They had organised a bus to go to the game,' said Bone. 'I don't think anyone on that bus was a Partick Thistle supporter, but they were Thistle fans for the day.'

As the 'Fallin faithful' await the arrival of their bus many will have been reading that morning's *Daily Record* where their hero has given an interview to the acclaimed writer Alex Cameron. Bone is pictured on the shoulder of his work-mates, each with hard hat and miner's lamp.

'I reckon we're pretty confident we can beat Celtic. Why shouldn't we?' Bone is quoted as saying in the article. 'It's a final, and it's 11 men against 11. Don't think we're over-confident. That would be crazy against a side with Celtic's record. I hope we all play well and that it is a good game to watch.'

Bone was catching a bus of his own that morning, one of the corporation variety.

Just six miles away in Tullibody, John Hansen is also up and about. He is staying with his in-laws as he and wife Sandra, newly married in June, squirrel away funds for a home of their own. His sleep has been hijacked too, by the thoughts of what lay ahead. A cup final. Against Celtic. And he is going head-to-head with Jimmy Johnstone.

What could you say about the diminutive Celtic winger? The greatest? Possibly. Certainly in the top two – and his only rival for that title, a certain Kenny Dalglish, is also playing this afternoon. It is little wonder that Hansen has found himself staring at the ceiling for much of the night.

'The night before the game I was just so nervous,' he said. 'Mainly because we were playing Celtic so we didn't give ourselves much of a chance let alone anybody else. You are just thinking hopefully we can keep the score down and we're not going to get slaughtered by them.

'Just two years before I was playing in the Combination League against teams like Glasgow Police and Glasgow Transport.' If one were setting off on the road to Hampden glory then Tullibody and Fallin are curious places from where to take a first step. But this is where it will begin for Hansen and Bone. Not the plush overnight hotel stays that the big names and the big teams are accustomed to. For them it is a bus journey shared with those nipping out to get the messages or the bookies to put on their line, heading out to the pub or popping round to Aunt Jean's for a visit. It is ordinary, so very ordinary.

The clock ticks by slowly and every minute the nerves seem to grow that little bit more, right up until the time they have to leave for the game. Sandra and John depart with little fanfare and head down the steep hill to the bus stop to await the service that will take them to Stirling train station, then onward to Queen Street in Glasgow and another bus stop wait before they reach the rest of the Partick Thistle team. If this is the glamour of life as a professional footballer then someone has a good sense of humour.

'It's bizarre to think about it now,' Hansen said. 'We got two buses and a train.'

Bone is making a similar journey. Often, he and Hansen would travel together but the passage of time dulls the memory. Did they do it on this day, 23 October 1971? One maintains they did; the other is not so sure.

What both agree on is that few people paid them any kind of notice.

'People didn't talk to us on the train,' Bone said. 'The thing about it was that everybody knew football players from a mile away because they all dressed the same. It would either be blazer, flannels and a club tie or it would be a suit and a club tie. You could spot them a mile away.'

As the train rattles its way towards Glasgow and closer and closer to a destiny neither Bone nor Hansen could possibly imagine, those passengers who barely give them a second glance could hardly be blamed for failing to engage with these gladiators in their midst. What could they possibly say other than a cursory 'good luck'? Had they offered up a voice predicting a Thistle victory the whole carriage would have known they were mad. Little wonder then that they are silent. For who on earth gives Thistle a chance?

* * *

ALAN ROUGH is standing at the side of the pitch opposite his home in the high flats on Lincoln Avenue in Knightswood. Things are not going well. For most of the game since the 10am kick-off the Boys' Brigade team he is coaching has been on the back foot and another heavy defeat is in the offing.

It is perhaps safe to say that the 237 Knightswood Battalion was not the strongest outfit when it came to the beautiful game. But Rough enjoyed the coaching and, at 19, the game was a welcome distraction ahead of what lay ahead that afternoon.

'We never won. I think we got beat about 8-0,' he said. 'The young BB boys were focusing on what they were doing. Some of the parents were saying "all the best this afternoon" but it was pretty low key.'

It would have been approaching noon by the time he returned to the flat where mum Jean tries to persuade him to sit down for what passed as a plate of protein in Glasgow in the '70s – bacon, sausages and eggs. But Rough knows he has a pre-match meal waiting for him when he meets up with the Partick Thistle team at Esquire House, just a short hop along nearby Great Western Road.

Jean, like all mums one must suppose, is anxious her boy has a good feed in his stomach.

'I had a big fight with my mum not to have my usual bacon, sausage and eggs which was the protein in our house before a game of football,' he said. 'I kept saying to her I was going for a pre-match meal, I don't need anything. And she was saying "oh get that in you".'

She is insistent but Rough wins the argument this time and busies himself checking his kit bag is packed correctly. Like many members of the goalkeeping union, Rough is a superstitious fellow. His gloves are there, with the stopwatch he would always keep in his hat and the lucky jumper. His boots and such like he knew would be coming with the rest of the kit from Firhill but the important items he trusts only to himself.

'I had all my stuff,' he said. 'I have always been quite superstitious about having my own stuff and looking after it. Any wee bits and bobs so I always had my own bag to take with me.

'I used to have my goalkeeping gloves and everything, things I was always a bit anxious wouldn't get packed. I always wore a lucky jersey so I always made sure I had that with me.

'My mum wasn't a big football fanatic. My dad was bursting my ears all the way out the door. "Have you got this and got that?" The usual dad stuff, making sure you were okay.'

Rough's choice of jacket provides another talking point. It has been around five years since The Kinks released their classic hit 'Dedicated Follower of Fashion' but the lyrics still resonate with the 19-year-old. A barrage of checks and flicks, it would have been enough to have given even Arthur Montford a touch of the vapours.

'They seek him here
They seek him there
His clothes are loud
But never square
It will make or break him so he's got to buy the best
'Cause he's a dedicated follower of fashion.'

'I can't believe that jacket,' Rough said. 'I don't know where that jacket came from. We were all trying to live up to [team-mate] John Gibson's fashion sense.

'He had the trendy hairstyle and always came in for games immaculate with a new suit or a trendy Ben Sherman shirt. It was just outrageous. It is hard to describe it. It was worse than the jackets Arthur Montford used to wear. It was worse than that. It was a multi colour of checks. I don't know why I would wear that to a cup final.'

Rough leaves the flat and heads down to the bus stop to await the arrival of the 11a from Drumchapel. He does not have to wait long but he notices that the bus is full, packed to the roof with Celtic fans. If he is wanting to remain incognito the choice of jacket is a gamble.

He boards the service and with no seats available downstairs he climbs the narrow stairs to the top level where he spies one single, unoccupied seat, about two from the front, and plonks himself down. The cup final goalkeeper is on the 11a bus heading along Great Western Road and not a single soul is giving him a second thought but for his dapper appearance.

'Most of the Celtic supporters coming from Drumchapel were on that bus,' Rough said. 'It was full of them and I am just sitting there. A lot of them are having a laugh at the jacket but nobody knew who I was anyway.

'We had just come up from the lower division, this was our first season and nobody knew the young boys then.'

The buzz as the bus moves off is all about 'the game'. Celtic are used to winning, Hampden is a second home and the confidence of the fans is well-placed. The theme of the chatter is not about 'how?' but 'how many?' But the atmosphere is friendly and positive and the Celtic fan alongside Rough turns to begin conversation.

'I'll never forget it,' Rough said. 'The guy had one of those big muffler scarves and a tammy on and his exact words to me were, "Where are you goin' the day, son?"

'I didn't want to delve into where I was going or anything like that so I said I was just going for a game of football but he kept asking me questions. "Is your team doing well an' that?" I said, "Aye, aye we're doing all right." It was just general Glasgow blethering. I wasn't brave enough to say, "Do you know who I am, do you know where I'm going?"

'I just sat there because the bus ride from Knightswood to Anniesland was only six or seven minutes. It was just football chat without delving in to where I was actually going.

'But his famous last words to me as I was getting off, I'll never forget it, he said, "All the best son, hope everything goes well for ye." And I'm thinking to myself, "I don't think you'll be saying that later on!"'

The bus by now has travelled through Anniesland Cross and passed under the railway bridge at the station. Rough crosses the road and up into Esquire House where the Thistle team are assembling. They share the restaurant with members of the general public and although their section is cordoned off there is little need. Few people pay them any notice.

'There were people coming and going but nothing was said,' Rough said. 'I remember I had a steak and chips. I don't know who was sitting next to me but they had steak and chips as well but they had only eaten half so I had the rest of it.'

Mum Jean would have been happy. He had, after all, passed up her sausage, bacon and eggs.

* * *

MANAGER Davie McParland has ensured everything in the build-up to the game remained the same for his players – and he has kept it as normal as possible at home as well. Inside, his heart may well have been racing, tactics whirling around his head, but on the outside he was a picture of calmness.

From the back windows of his house in Roselea Drive, Milngavie he could look out towards the Mugdock and Craigmaddie reservoirs. It was a place he knew well given the amount of times he had jogged around them as he prepared for pre-season. It was the perfect family home, perfect for daughters Yvonne, Tracy and Hazel to grow up, playing in the back fields that offered some peace and quiet from the rigours of management.

As he looks out over the picturesque scene despite the rain in the air he wonders what the day might hold.

'As a child we didn't really notice much but in the run-up to the game he was as cool as a cucumber,' said daughter Yvonne. 'Everything running up to the game was just a normal week. He wasn't anything out of the ordinary on the morning – in particular he didn't change any routine. It was just up as normal, just another day. You imagine that inside he might have been thinking differently but he didn't feel, look or act any differently in front of us.'

Ordinarily Yvonne, at 12 the eldest of the three, would be heading for the football but today it is different. She has chosen to stay at home with her sisters with Auntie Vera looking after the trio.

'I was nervous,' said Yvonne. 'I would have hated to have gone and they didn't win it, hated it for my dad. I have no regrets in life except for that one but to be fair it was still a magical day for us, it was something I shouldn't have missed.'

Terry McParland is certainly determined to be there, the supporting wife as always through triumph and despair. She will be joining the rest of the wives and partners at their own pre-match meal the club are laying on at Firhill. With the house full of the usual family hustle and bustle it is the domestic chores that are keeping everyone busy. That and the scanning of the morning papers, the majority of which see only one outcome in the afternoon's encounter. McParland is untroubled by the predictions. It suits his game plan, further proof if needed that so many have forgotten how capable and talented his side is.

Terry is happy to allow her husband to prepare in his own way. But she is insistent on just one thing.

'My mum used to dress my dad beautifully,' said Yvonne. 'He had an extensive wardrobe and he wore his clothes brilliantly but she insisted he wear a suit and the same shirt and tie for every League Cup game right up to the final. So, she sent him away in his nice blue suit, shirt and tie. She was very superstitious, he most certainly was not.

'Like all good men he did what his wife told him.'

McParland kisses each of his daughters goodbye as he and Terry depart. They will be separated from each other soon enough, each going in a different direction but heading for the same venue and the same date with destiny. Terry will meet up at Firhill with other wives and partners, McParland with his players at their usual pre-match haunt.

* * *

By now other Thistle players have assembled inside the bowels of Esquire House. Denis McQuade has 'jetted' in from the family home in Dennistoun in his pride and joy – a Ford Cortina 1600E. Not bad for a student at the University of Glasgow studying Mathematics and French. His brother Tommy had travelled with him in order to take the car back.

'I do remember having steak,' said McQuade. 'That's probably the worst thing you can eat before a match but that was the Thistle tradition.'

Captain Alex Rae has travelled on the train from Paisley Gilmour Street and got a taxi to Esquire House but he did not travel alone.

'There were a couple of youngsters I used to kid on who lived near me, both Celtic supporters – about 14 and 12 – nice young guys,' he said. 'I met them on the train, we had a good blether and of course they asked me how I thought we would get on today. Without any hesitation I said, "I think we'll win today," so they both had a good chuckle at that.'

Rae joins the Thistle dining party but there is no steak for him.

'It was business as normal,' he said. 'Big Alan Rough will tell you he had a steak and all that carry-on. He's a blether. We had the usual, just basic, something very simple.'

Full-back Alex Forsyth had spent the morning walking his father's greyhounds near the family home in Baillieston before heading back home for some tea and toast. His dad would give him a lift to meet up with the team.

His thoughts are dominated by the game and the prospect of facing one of the greatest players Scotland have, or will ever, produce.

Jimmy Johnstone was simply world-class. He seemed to play with the ball glued to his feet, twisting and turning, tying a defender in knots before doubling back to do it all again. He could make a fool of an opposition player and, at just

19 years of age, Forsyth will be one of the Thistle rear-guard tasked with stopping him. It is a frightening proposition but Forsyth's laid back character is a huge asset in this situation.

'I walked the dogs in the morning as usual,' Forsyth said. 'My dad had about two or three greyhounds. I was thinking about the game, trying to take it all in and thinking about what was going to happen that day. It was fantastic. I was only 19. When you are young like that you don't really fear anything. As you get older it's worse but I was of the view that if things go well on the day then all well and good.

'I had Jimmy Johnstone to cope with and I was thinking, "How am I going to play him, what am I going to do?" I wondered if I was going to kick him or just play him normal. Everything is going through your mind. Is he going to take the mickey out of you? What am I going to do to stop it?

'I was definitely nervous but not so nervous that I couldn't concentrate for the final. I'm quite a laid back kind of person anyway.'

Johnstone's roving commission meant he was to be a problem not just for Forsyth but for the entire Thistle back four. There was just no way to nullify him, short of an injury that would remove him from the fray of course.

John Hansen, Thistle's other young full-back, also has Johnstone front and centre in his mind.

'The worst thing about playing against Jimmy was that I really liked him,' Hansen said. 'Normally you would try to intimidate wingers or kick them or something but Jimmy was such a nice wee guy. And you knew, well I knew, how he was going to get past me. And he knew how he was going to get past me.

'You just couldn't stop him, he just jinked and jinked and he just waited for you moving forward and when you moved forward to him then that is when he went past you.

'He had this habit that when he went past you, he would come back and say, "Come on John, try again, try harder this time." And I used to say to him, "Jimmy just fuck off, you've beaten me don't try and beat me again."

'And he'd say "but you might get me this time". Normally if a winger played like that you would deck him but with him it was like "Jimmy, just please go away". He was just such a nice guy that you just couldn't kick him.'

Frank Coulston has arrived from Bishopbriggs where he is the PE teacher at the local high school. Perhaps he is reflecting on how his fortunes have changed. Just the season before he had looked as if he was heading out of Firhill, struggling for game time and failing to be a fixture in the first team. He had asked for a free transfer but had been told by Davie McParland to keep the faith. Coulston took his manager's words on board. Now he is just hours from starting in the League Cup Final.

Jackie Campbell, too, has reason to marvel at the fickle finger of fate. He had not played many games under McParland in the previous season as he battled back from injury and then couldn't get back into a side that was on its way to winning the Second Division title. In fact, he still felt bad that the season previous to that he had been unable to help Scot Symon from keeping Thistle in the top flight as he once again succumbed to injuries.

'I felt really aggrieved as well because the year before I hadn't played a lot, I had been injured, and I feel I let Scot Symon down in a way because he was always wanting me to play but I never really made it back to full fitness for him,' Campbell said. 'I had a good relationship with him and Willie Thornton before him.

'I didn't play many games at all. I had been injured and because the team was doing well then Mr McParland didn't want to chop it and change it. I didn't play many games and when I did play I played at left-back.

'I thought at that time I was going to find it difficult to find a way back in but then as things go you get on the training pitch and, because I had played with Davie previously, he had faith in me and knew what I was capable of. As things progressed, I played a few games at the end of the season after recovering from the injury and the next year it picked up again. He was looking for experience to complement the young ones going into the First Division at that time.'

So now Campbell was back as a fixture in the side – and he was confident. The morning has been spent with wife Jean dropping off their three kids – all under six

– with grandparents. The wives and girlfriends were to be entertained with lunch at Firhill before heading to Hampden.

As he drove Jean towards Maryhill before going on to join up with his team-mates he turned to her.

'I said "we are going to win today",' said Campbell, who had worked all week as a contracts manager at a steel company – another of Thistle's part-time soldiers. 'It is an attitude of mind. I just believed that we had the capabilities, we had the will and the want to go and win.'

The players depart their hostelry and head out into the October air. The rain that has been falling is lighter now and hopefully it will be dry come kick-off. They know the pitch will be slick. Perhaps that will play into their hands. Time will tell.

Those passing by and walking down Great Western Road, and those peering out from the windows of Esquire House, pay them little by way of attention. Inside, a single television flickers in the background. It, too, is failing to grab anyone's attention.

The BBC's *Football Focus* programme is coming to an end. Presenter Sam Leitch is running through the football agenda of the day.

'And in Scotland it's League Cup Final day,' he says. 'It's Celtic against Partick Thistle – who have no chance.'

* * *

In the quiet Clackmannanshire village of Sauchie, just outside Alloa, 15-year-old Alan Hansen is climbing into the car with his dad and his uncle. They have seen every game of Thistle's journey to Hampden this season, revelling in the performance of Alan's big brother John at right-back. Normally they are confident but today they travel in hope rather than expectation.

'I went with my dad and my uncle from Sauchie where we lived,' Hansen said. 'John had left and was married by that time. So, I would have seen him on the Friday night and given him the usual good luck message.

'We went there on the morning of the game and got parked up. It was exciting because it was Hampden, there was a big crowd and you are playing one of the best teams in the world. I had seen them play in virtually every match in that run and I would go with my old man to see John play.

'For a 15-year-old kid it was unbelievably exciting – even before the game started never mind when it started. You want them to do well and I want John to do well. I was old enough and knew enough about the game to know good from bad or indifferent but we had no expectation, nobody had any expectation of Thistle winning and what was to follow was one of the biggest turn ups in footballing history.

'Thistle were a good attacking team that could score goals and you had my brother at right-back who was a good attacking player and Alex Forsyth on the other side who was quick and could get forward. Alex could shoot as well so you had a lot of gunfire, you had people who could score goals and a team that could score goals. But that didn't matter on the day because you are up against Celtic who, in 1971, were as good as it gets.'

* * *

The Thistle team bus heads out into the busy Saturday traffic and plots its way to the national stadium from the north of the city, crossing the river and heading towards Mount Florida.

The mood is quiet. Normally it is more jovial than this, laughs and jokes and a card school up the back. But there is little by way of chatter.

Midfielder Ronnie Glavin is reflecting on a troubling couple of weeks not knowing if the ankle injury, which has seen him miss games against St Johnstone and Dunfermline, would also keep him out of the big one. In training just days before he had gone into a full challenge and emerged intact. The ankle had held up.

'I wasn't sure I was going to be playing,' Glavin said. 'I trained on the Thursday and I went through a challenge. As I got up the manager asked me how I was feeling, how the ankle was. I told him it was good and I knew then I would be in the squad so I was happy. I didn't know if I was going to be playing but I'll tell you what, if I was to be playing I was sure I was going to be ready for it. I just couldn't wait to get going.

'I thought to myself if I'm playing I'm going to run my blood to water in this game. I didn't care, it didn't matter to me and the boys were of the same opinion. When you come from where we came from, what have we got to lose?'

As it turned out, Glavin was to start and play an integral role alongside Alex Rae. He was also to have a hand, or a boot, in a key moment in the first half. But that is for the future. For now, he is in determined mood.

'I remember the night before the cup final I went for a game of snooker with a pal, John Green, who was a mad Celtic fan,' said Glavin. 'The people where I come from were fantastic but as we were walking to get the bus to go to the snooker hall one of the guys shouts over, "Hey, Glav, 6-0 or 7-0 for Celtic, we'll hammer you tomorrow." I said, "Oh it's going to be that easy is it?" And he replied, "Aye, you'll all shite yourselves and you'll no' try!"

'Well, that's one thing I would never do so I told him to pay his money and see if I try or not.

'I remember John standing up for me, saying he'd rather see me win a medal than Jimmy Johnstone winning a medal and he was a Celtic fan.

'I was fuming. I was so annoyed by this guy. I was also encouraged because John was a mad Celtic fan but supporting me.'

The vista has changed now as the bus rolls on towards Mount Florida. The quiet pavements and relaxed atmosphere of earlier have gone to be replaced by the noise of chatter and cheers. Looking out the window the Thistle players are met with smiling faces of expectation. Soon the hundreds have turned into thousands, a sea of green and white and red and yellow.

'I don't think you realise you are at a cup final until you get near Hampden,' said Alan Rough. 'As soon as the bus turns the corner you see the supporters and then it really hits home.

'I always felt later on in my career that was a big part of having to handle the pressure of big games. Dealing with what was walking along the road and the smiling supporters and the expectancy of winning and losing. It is a happy moment but it just really sinks in. You see your supporters and Celtic supporters.'

The final part of the journey, turning from Mount Florida towards the stadium, is rough and ready. A simple dirt track road that has the bus bouncing as it plots its way to the door. But the stadium is in front of them now. Destiny awaits.

'The good thing from my point of view, and certainly from the young boys' point of view, was that we had been to Hampden before,' said Rough. 'I had never been before we played Falkirk in the semi-final, [but now] we had been in the dressing room and played on the park.

'It made a big difference from just turning up on the day and being in awe. Going there in the semi-final was a big thing for me. It was a fantastic occasion. I mean, I hear a lot of people saying now we should switch it to Murrayfield or Pittodrie but not for me. That is what you play football for, to play at the national stadium.'

Jackie Campbell may be one of the experienced hands in Davie McParland's side but he too is feeling the nervous tension as the bus navigates the final part of its journey.

'The amount of people getting nearer to Hampden. I mean I had played in games at Firhill with Rangers and Celtic where there was 25,000 but we were going to Hampden and we just didn't appreciate the volume that would be there,' he said. 'It was just a continual build-up. The nearer you got the heavier the flow of people and fans going to the ground. Then getting there and getting into the stadium and going out on to the pitch you see it starting to fill up and then you find out there is 62,000 there which is unbelievable.'

Denis McQuade lifts a hand to wave to some of the Thistle fans tripping over themselves to get a glimpse of their team. He is nervous, but is in control of his emotions.

'The semi-final was important because Hampden is a big park and at least we got familiar with it,' he said. 'Having a good experience there, it took away the mystique and the Hampden aura and all the things you dream about as a young fellow wanting to play there.

'It certainly made us relax a bit more, going into the final knowing that we had come though a good game there.'

John Hansen too is in awe of the crowd, the sea of humanity that is emerging before him.

'The mood on the bus, it was fairly quiet and sedate because you are seeing all these people, all the crowd and you're thinking, "Jesus Christ, what have we got ourselves into here?" All the time you are thinking it's Celtic, I mean if it had been anybody else. You think, "What am I doing here? I'm a wee boy from Sauchie."

'You see all these people and when you look at the crowd and compare it to the biggest crowd we would have played [in front of] before it must have been a magnitude of ten for the final. Our crowds, okay you maybe played Rangers and Celtic at their grounds, but it was nothing like 62,000.'

McParland rises from his seat towards the front of the bus and turns to face his players. He knows they have been written off by everyone, that it is a foregone conclusion, that Celtic only have to turn up to win and lift yet another piece of silverware. He knows the size of the task his players face and the challenge they must rise to come 3pm and kick-off.But he also knows his team. They have prepared well. They are fit and focused and confident. They are the perfect mix of youth and experience. And, what is more, they are playing well. If Thistle are being written off then it suits him just fine. Because people have forgotten that his team can play a bit.

As the doors of the bus prepare to open he looks at his players once more and tells them, 'You are not here today to make up the numbers; it is not a given that Celtic will beat you. You CAN win the League Cup.'

'If you don't go into any game with that attitude, you might as well stay at home,' McParland would recall later. 'I don't know if the players believed me but I had to get them revved up.'

CHAPTER 6

THE OPPOSITION

THE wind is whistling in from the Firth of Clyde and gusting across the beach, kicking up sand as it blows towards Seamill. This quiet, picturesque spot which bumps shoulder to shoulder with West Kilbride is nearly 50 miles from Parkhead but it is a lifetime away from the goldfish bowl in which Celtic Football Club exists. It is why Celtic are here.

From the beach, across the water and the waves, the southern aspect of Arran is clear and, further to the south, Ailsa Craig pokes its head over the horizon. Dogs are being quietly walked in front of the Seamill Hydro Hotel, chasing sticks and galloping into the water. It is peaceful. Little wonder it had been the choice of many over the years seeking to recharge their batteries.

Jock Stein had been a passionate advocate of the venue as the place to take his team, a key part of their build-up for the biggest of games. As players said, then and now, if you were at Seamill you immediately knew it was a big game – and everybody had to be on it.

In truth Celtic had been travelling to this oasis of calm since the days of Jimmy McGrory taking his players to 'their favourite Seamill haunt' in the late 1940s.

Celtic had travelled down on the Thursday just a day after putting five past Maltese minnows Sliema Wanderers in the second round of the European Cup.

'We aren't doing anything about the final just now,' says Jock Stein, although the game is now only days away. 'Billy McNeill isn't 100 per cent fit but we are hoping he will be ready.

'We'll get on with selecting the side on Friday after we've settled down from the Sliema match.'

There is a light training session on the lawn in front of the hotel. It is a curious sight with balls often being kicked over the large stone wall that separates the hotel from the beach. Young kids scramble to retrieve them, desperately racing back to return them to these legends in their midst.

Sometimes, training would take place on the beach itself. But it was never a high-intensity workout. These thoroughbreds were at their peak and the point of the stay was more to keep engines ticking over and minds focused and away from the attention and distractions of the big city.

The players would room in pairs and each morning, before breakfast, they would gather in the foyer and head out for a stroll just to keep the blood flowing in the legs. They would head out on to the main road and turn left towards West Kilbride before heading down by the golf course and along a lane that led them to the beach. Then it was back along the sand and to the hotel.

The morning of the League Cup Final was exactly like that. A quiet stroll, some sea air in the lungs, breakfast and then relax.

To pass them on their morning exercise was to rub shoulders with giants. The names trip of the tongue. Bobby Murdoch, Jimmy Johnstone, Tommy Gemmell, Billy McNeill, Bobby Lennox were all remnants of the Lisbon Lions 1967 side that was the envy of Europe. But there was new blood coming into the team from a goldmine reserve side which was to become known as the Quality Street Gang. George Connelly, Lou Macari, Davie Hay, Paul Wilson and Kenny Dalglish were legends of the future but already stars of today.

Many of them had already crossed Partick Thistle before – kind of. In 1968 Celtic needed a seven-goal triumph over Thistle if they were to beat rivals Rangers in their Reserve League Cup section. They won 12-0 with Macari scoring four goals.

Two months later, after then-Scotland boss Bobby Brown had asked Stein to supply opposition for a practice match, Celtic sent their Quality Street Gang. The beat the full Scottish international side 5-2.

So, this Celtic team, walking peacefully along the shore, is in transition. But it is still a side of winners. The pain of missing out on a second European Cup when they underestimated Feyenoord in the final the year before was still there. They had gone out to Ajax in the quarter-finals the following season in a tie that again could be looked upon as a missed opportunity.

But Stein was building again, developing a team with which titles and silverware became common bedfellows.

'The morning after Lisbon, Stein sat down with Jimmy Gordon and gave an interview in which he said "we can't look back, we must look forward",' said Archie Macpherson. 'They went on to play in a friendly game with Real Madrid for Di Stéfano and Stein, determined not to play his Lisbon team, made changes. He didn't want them to be playing the team that won the European Cup just in case Real beat them. Stein was a man of great sensitivity and pride and in fact Celtic won 1-0.

'It was a transition game [against Thistle] and maybe in a sense that affected Celtic. For some of them it might have been an early cup final but dominant they were that is for sure.

'In '67 they had a clean sweep European Cup and everything else, league, League Cup, Scottish Cup and everything else so in that respect they gained such momentum and status that it was going to be very difficult for any team to beat them.

'The only club who could do that would be Rangers but they even dominated Rangers in that period. So, when we get to the '71 period they were very strong favourites and really nobody expected Thistle to do anything. I mean Celtic had strong players and you were beginning to see a new generation of players, they were moving away from Lisbon. Davie Hay was emerging in the team, the highly talented George Connelly was in the side, Dalglish was beginning to make his mark at that time and players who were in and out like Harry Hood, Tommy Callaghan and of course the very colourful Lou Macari.

'The team that played at Hampden that day was in the transition if you like. Halfway through a significant transition into a different period. So, it was a significant day.'

Just a year before, Stein had wrestled with the dilemma of what to do with his Lions. They couldn't go on for ever and in 1970 he decided to break up the side. It was partly because of what he had said in that interview, about the constant need for change and evolution, but also because of the faith he had in the fledgling starlets who were emerging from the shadows and into the light.

In his book *The Quality Street Gang – The Greatest Team That Never Was*, author Paul John Dykes writes:

'How do you replace such an iconic captain and leader of men as Billy McNeill, who possessed all the natural qualities of a born winner? Or a winger of such supreme individual talent and panache as Jimmy Johnstone, whose strength and mesmerising dribbling ability bamboozled defences all over the world? Or the commanding and peerlessly influential and talismanic Bobby Murdoch, who could pass the ball with a range and precision that could orchestrate an entire match? These were just some of the dilemmas that faced Jock Stein but the breaking up of this incredible Lisbon Lions dynasty was made a lot smoother by the sheer raft of talent that was waiting in the wings.

'Despite the phenomenal success of his team over the previous few seasons, Jock Stein had possessed the foresight to plan ahead and had signed a procession of prodigious Scottish talents, who had been learning their trade from the very best in European football on the Barrowfield training ground every day since their arrival at the club. Inconspicuous young men whose indoctrination into the Celtic way had been gradual and methodical. These young cubs were reared to replace the Lisbon Lions, the most celebrated football team in the history of the Scottish game.

'Jock Stein almost simultaneously crafted two football teams in the late 1960s and early '70s, that would ensure Celtic could enjoy utter dominance of the Scottish game for virtually a decade.'

Some of the old guard could read the warning signs. John Hughes and Willie Wallace had departed for Crystal Palace just days before the Hampden meeting with Thistle. For football is a beast that never stands still, it is constantly evolving, constantly changing. Nothing lasts for ever.

'It was the future, the team was going through a wee bit of a transition,' said Jim Craig. 'But in a very short space of time that team was winning things as well.'

* * *

For many, if not all, of this Thistle side, facing Celtic will be a new experience. For they are a side in transition too. The young players who have been blooded in the side in the Second Division are still finding their feet in the top league. But they are doing so with gusto. Just ask the Rangers team who were defeated 3-2 in the opening league game of the campaign at Firhill.

As the Celtic bus pulls out of Seamill and makes its way along the coast and to Hampden, the Thistle players do not fear its arrival.

'See when you look back, at the time Celtic were so prominent in Europe and had probably the greatest ever manager in history in Jock Stein at the helm. You are talking a serious situation that you are up against,' said Ronnie Glavin.

'But I wasn't frightened. I didn't care, it didn't matter to me and the boys were of the same opinion.'

'Jock Stein was clearly blending something as well with the experience and the young players but we were probably ahead in terms of gelling too,' said Frank Coulston. 'When we went into the final, I can't remember being worried about it, I was looking forward to it. Just play as you can play and we had been playing well for over a season and more so there was no real fear. The way we played was no surprise.'

And Thistle have good reason to feel they can pull off a shock, for they will be playing without pressure. The newspapers, the commentators, the pundits can see no other outcome than a Celtic win. Some have couched it in such a way as to offer Thistle the slimmest of chances. But it reads like a get-out card.

The newspapers are being passed around the bus as the Celtic players kill time on the journey to Glasgow. Someone tosses a *Shoot!* magazine on to a seat and it falls open at the cup final preview spread. 'CELTIC TO BEAT THISTLE IN A THRILLER', it cries.

'Mighty Celtic, hailed by their fans as the greatest show on earth, go on the trophy trail again when they play in their EIGHTH successive Scottish League Cup Final,' it reads.

'Jock Stein's men for all seasons have won the trophy five times in their previous seven on-the-trot attempts and their final opponents at Hampden, Partick Thistle, have been well-warned that Celtic have their goal-sights on bringing in League Cup number six.

'Celtic, the most powerful goal machine Scotland has ever known, are confident they can keep up their amazing run of success.

'Thistle will face a 90 minutes of trying to out-think one of the most lethal and goal-hungry teams in the country. It is a task that may prove to be too much for the Firhill men. They will fight as they have done in earlier rounds … they will attack also, but they could find themselves with too much to do.'

The Celtic eyes which perhaps scanned the article have every reason to agree with its premise. But there are others who reason differently, and there is evidence to back up their argument. This Celtic team is not infallible, it is not without weakness. Morton and St Johnstone have both beaten them already this season.

'I just believed that we would win that day,' said Jackie Campbell. 'But the Celtic team was a great team, it hadn't fully broken up but there were younger players coming in so they were in a transition as well but we had come up into the First Division and were playing well so we had confidence in our own ability to go and compete with them.

'It was not long after they had won the European Cup. Dalglish had broken through, Macari and Hay, and George Connelly was a great player. That team was in transition but they were still a very good team because the backbone of the Lisbon team was still there.

'Celtic, it didn't matter when you played them, it was the same as Rangers, you always felt as if you were playing against 12 men. They were full-timers, I was part-time, I knew there was a difference in the stature and they had more legs than we had. You could never relax even if you were in front of them with two minutes to go because they would always come back at you. That was just how they played the game.

'They had a really good team and we should not have had a chance against them in a sense. But I believed from the week before it that we would win. They were writing us off in the papers that they were just needing to turn up and they would be getting a winner's medal but we had a belief in ourselves that we had made it to the final and we would go and attack them.'

At the front of the bus, Jock Stein has has to come to terms with the absence of his talismanic captain in his line-up for the afternoon. The groin injury that had kept Billy McNeill out of European action just days before has not recovered in time. Stein has decided to gamble and push George Connelly back from his midfield berth.

He has total faith in the 12 names he had written on the piece of paper in his top pocket although the players were made aware of his selection the night before.

Evan Williams, Tommy Gemmell, Connelly, Jim Brogan, Davie Hay; Bobby Murdoch (captain), Jimmy Johnstone, Harry Hood, Tommy Callaghan, Lou Macari and Kenny Dalglish. The experience of Jim Craig would be on the bench.

And then there is Stein himself, this colossus of a manager. Arguably the greatest ever. Even Alex Ferguson described working under him as taking an honours degree in management. This is the man who had arrived at Celtic in 1965 and transformed a basket case of a club into the kings of Europe. As Bobby Murdoch said, 'Jock Stein saved Celtic.' Now, with his new breed, he is hoping to do it all again. They are behind him, physically, of course, but metaphorically too. Pristine, like new pins in their club blazers ready to do whatever their master decreed.

The journey is nearing its end. For so many on the Celtic bus this sojourn to Hampden has become almost second nature and the national stadium a second home. When they had left Seamill a small pocket of fans had cheered and waved them off. Here, as the bus makes its way towards Mount Florida, the crowd falling off the pavement and out on to the road is huge, boisterous and buoyant. The smiling players wave. They are relaxed simply because they have a lot to be relaxed about and there is no need for Stein to give them any pep talk.

As they turn into the confines of the stadium, with the buzz of the final carrying in the air, they notice that the Thistle bus is already there.

CHAPTER 7

THE ARRIVAL

AS the doors of the Thistle bus open to allow the players and coaching staff to spill out, Alan Rough looks through the crowd and spots his father's well-kent face staring back at him.

'It was always a panic if he never got his two complimentary tickets,' Rough said as he recalled his father Bob's pre-match antics. 'At Hampden there was a wee window where you got your tickets. You put them in an envelope and you left them there. My dad was always panicking because anybody could go up and say "Alan Rough tickets" and it happened to a couple of people so he was always paranoid that he got his tickets.'

In future years Bob's fear about losing tickets would reach new extremes. When his son was firmly in situ as Scotland's number one it even saw him breach the sanctity of the home dressing room.

'We were playing against Holland at Hampden and Jock Stein, the manager, was getting ready for a team talk, maybe 35 minutes before the start of the game,' Rough said. 'A wee security guard popped his head round the door and said, "Mr Stein, can I speak to Alan Rough?"

'He pointed me out in the dressing room and this security guard tells me that my dad can't find his tickets. I told him to go back and tell them I had left them in the box. Fifteen minutes later my dad walks into the dressing room – I don't know how he got by all the stewards. "Excuse me Mr Stein," he says, "can I speak to my son?" He's got his tartan bunnet and his tartan scarf. Joe Jordan and Kenny Dalglish are looking, wondering what is going on. And lo and behold I hadn't put the tickets out – they were in my inside pocket. So, I gave him the tickets and he's away saying "sorry aboot that!" For now, those Hampden nights that would become such a regular occurrence in the Rough household seem a lifetime away. At just 19 years of age this is only a second trip to the home of Scottish football for the young goalkeeper. As the Thistle team file into the stadium the magnitude of what awaits them begins to dawn on some. For others the innocence of youth is a defence.

'Leading up to it we were all quite relaxed because nobody thought we were going to win,' said Rough. 'And that must include us as well. Being the underdogs there was no pressure on you.'

They march in, through the main doors and turn left into the home dressing room. It is an oasis of calm, of solitude away from the growing noise outside as the atmosphere builds towards kick-off. It was different to what many of the Thistle team were used to.

'The dressing room was spanking,' said Rough. 'All brand-new mahogany. It looked like a golf club locker room. You could get your whole jacket and trousers in the locker whereas at most other clubs you just had a peg. There was a wee bit for your shoes. And there was a treatment room behind glass. It was immaculate.'

Rough takes his seat beside full-backs Alex Forsyth and John Hansen. The young crowd. Bodies, team-mates, back-room staff continue to file in. It's getting crowded now. The nervous energy coursing through them means they do not sit for long. They are bouncing and are desperate to get going, like thoroughbreds ahead of a race.

Davie McParland has worked hard all week trying to keep things as normal as possible. Training hasn't changed. He thought long and hard about taking the team away for a few days but had learned a lesson from bitter experience.

'He had experienced two finals in the past and lost both of them,' said Ronnie Glavin. 'On each occasion they went away for a few days to prepare for the cup final and then come the game, the legs were left at the seaside. Davie had said he didn't want that to happen so he kept it as normal a week as possible. Did everything exactly the same, didn't change anything and it was good. There was a lot of talk about the way Celtic prepare and go away before the cup final. We were just keeping things on an even keel.'

But McParland has been keeping an eye on the media coverage in the build-up to the game. The newspapers have written Thistle off. McParland has kept his powder dry. He's happy that expectations surrounding his team are so low. Dismissed across the board except in the one place that matters – in the Thistle dressing room with the minutes ticking down. He keeps it calm but he also has a trick or two up his sleeve.

'I do remember when we went into the dressing room Davie had pinned an article up on the wall,' said Glavin. 'It said that the cup final is a mismatch, that you have 11 good-looking young lads with long hair strolling about trying to challenge the great might of this Celtic team. We pinned that up.

'The hairs on the back of your neck were standing up. It inspired us. Football is like that. I've experienced that on numerous occasions. It gets you buzzing, it gets you going, it gets your adrenalin going. That was an example of getting us ready. That was probably the start of it. We were so fired up it wasn't true.'

Some of the players take the opportunity to kill some time by taking a walk on the pitch. Bobby Lawrie sees a well-known face among the Celtic party. He and Lou Macari had grown up together in Kilwinning. They had gone to adjoining schools. The Celtic man spots Lawrie and they exchange pleasantries. Macari signs off by telling his pal, 'Och well, at least you'll get a runners-up medal.' 'That didn't go down too well with me,' said Lawrie. 'I went in and told the boys and they were raging. I think it helped us in the long run.'

The Celtic team sheet has appeared in the dressing room and confirms the glaring omission of captain Billy McNeill. Such a loss is a huge boost to Thistle hopes.

'Davie McParland came with the news that McNeill's not playing,' said Jimmy Bone. 'He told us that will take away a lot from their game. He wasn't decrying the players that were coming in, he just felt that McNeill was such a big part of Celtic, their leader.

'He told Frank [Coulston] and I to impose ourselves on the game. "Run the centre-backs now, you'll be too quick for them. Your pace will cause them problems. Just make sure you keep making the runs."

He was very positive in how he wanted us to play.

'Davie was a very calm manager. He had a really good football brain. He knew what you were going through because he had played for so long himself. He was very much a hands-on manager. He knew the players, he knew the individuals. He came up, just a wee quiet word. "They won't be as dominant in the air so you'll win your fair share of headers." All it does is it makes you feel that little bit bigger, that little bit better.'

McParland takes winger Denis McQuade aside. 'Your job is to mark Bobby Murdoch,' he tells him. 'When Celtic have the ball, I want you to be in touching distance of him because he is the engine of the team. If he doesn't get the ball then they don't have a creative flair. He is the most creative player in the team.'

'He always gave a lot of thought to what he was trying to convey,' McQuade said. 'If you look at any of the footage I am never very far away from Murdoch.'

'Try and keep Murdoch from getting the ball,' McParland tells him again. 'And when we have the ball by all means do what you think you need to do to make a difference.'

The tension is building now. All around the dressing room it is a flash of colour, of yellow and red.

'Later in my career I was always laughing and joking but I don't remember laughing and joking that day,' said Alan Rough.

'The young players were just focusing on the game and listening to what Alex Rae or Davie McParland was saying. Just taking it all in more than anything else.

'It was quiet. McParland had a presence as soon as he walked in, he had the respect of us all. We knew what to expect and I suppose the team talk would be very thorough. I wouldn't think for a minute it wouldn't have been. It was just like any big game you just want to get out there and get started.'

Now it is the manager's moment. The minutes before the dressing room door opens and he sends his team out hoping they will remember his instructions, follow them through and not be overawed by the occasion.

But McParland is not one for Churchillian oratory. It is not his style. Instead, he uses the silence and chooses his words carefully.

'You've done everything, you've trained and you're fit, just go and play,' he tells them. 'You know what you need to do. If you go and score goals they will need to come at you. You will have your good moments and your bad moments but just go and believe in yourselves.

'Look where we were and where we are now. You're professional footballers, you've done well to get where you are, just go out and enjoy yourselves.'

'McParland's major message to us was to give it a go,' said Denis McQuade. 'To go for them and we did. That is why we were successful because we did run at them.'

'I had heard it so many times that it was down to basics,' said Alex Rae. 'To do what you need to do, do it well, be it passes or tracking back. It was very simple and very easily understood, which for me is how it should be. I'm a straightforward guy and that was how I liked it. He talked us up, there is no question about that, and we went on to the park definitely thinking we had a chance.'

Such responsibility rested on Rae's shoulders. Captain, of course, but also one of the experienced heads keeping the youngsters around him grounded.

'The sensation was getting greater and greater, it is gradually building up, the realisation that battle is going to commence,' Rae said.

CHAPTER 8

THE FIRST HALF

THE bell tolls and echoes around the dressing room. It is time. The Thistle players make their last-minute check on boots, socks, studs. Perhaps there is a slapping of a back or two. A 'good luck, son' or 'right, let's do this'. Inside, each and every one of them is remembering his own job and what they have to do for the team. The instructions Davie McParland had given them in the days and hours before the kick-off; little snippets of information are now rattling around anxious heads.

'As we left the dressing room we just wished each other the best,' Bone said. 'The older guys, Alex Rae and Frank [Coulston] were geeing everyone up and the younger guys were just ready trying to build themselves up.

'I was really nervous before the game,' John Hansen said. 'Then when you went out, you're nervous but when the game starts you can't hear anything, it's just a blur.'

There is the clatter of studs on the white marble floor and in the background the sound of the crowd. As the door opens the noise grows louder, carrying up the stairs that will take them down to the pitch.

Alex Rae is at the front of the Thistle line, then Alan Rough, Frank Coulston, Jimmy Bone, Jackie Campbell, then Hansen. Others such as Denis McQuade and Hugh Strachan are filing in at the back. The captain takes one, two deep breaths. No sign of nerves. Don't show any sense of weakness. Lead.

'It is fantastic, the only word I could use,' said Rae. 'What a privilege. Was I nervous? I definitely had an edge but not a negative energy. I really felt as if I could run forever that day.

'I suppose different people when faced with a situation they might crumble but I'm afraid I wasn't one of them. It was an opportunity that I was happy to take on.'

'I remember that the two dressing rooms were opposite one another,' Alan Rough said. 'So, when the bell rang you came out and it was steps all the way down, it wasn't like that walkway. You were quite high up and you had to walk down all the steps and then you came out.

'When you came out the dressing room you couldn't see anything but you could hear the noise, you never saw anything until you got down the bottom.'

The Celtic team is already lined up, waiting. Their green and white strips are pristine and the players wearing them legends or legends in the making. At the front, leading them out is Bobby Murdoch. So, it's true, Billy McNeill isn't playing, the team lines didn't lie. There is little doubt that this is a huge boost to the underdogs but for some the Celtic supporting cast is still something to fear.

'There had been an interview with the two captains together on the Friday and we went for a coffee somewhere but at no stage did Billy mention that he wouldn't be playing,' said Rae. 'That is understandable. I was surprised but it didn't affect me. If anything, Billy McNeill being in the team or not in the team, I know which one I would prefer. That was a positive for me that it was Bobby Murdoch leading their team out.'

'Billy didn't play because he was carrying an injury,' said Celtic defender Jim Craig. 'I always wonder afterwards, if we were playing somebody other than Partick Thistle, might he have played? Was it because we were playing Partick Thistle, we might have said we can do without him here at this point?'

'When the dressing rooms come out Alex was first and I was second and they had already lined up,' Rough said. 'And they had the big stars. They had wee Jinky [Jimmy Johnstone], Tommy Gemmell. But I don't remember thinking "oh no, we shouldn't be here". The youth side of me kicked in because you never knew what was going to happen. That Celtic team – they had been European champions and we hadn't played them because we were in the lower division. I don't think we ever worried about them. It was about us really.'

But there was a gulf in class, surely? A Celtic team that was arguably the best in the land and contenders in Europe against a newly promoted ensemble of youth and part-time conscripts.

'You still thought of them as in a different league from you,' Hansen said. 'We didn't look upon ourselves a world-beaters or anything and even the people who came on to replace people like Billy [McNeill], we never thought we were in the same league as them.

'They were a phenomenal team. That was around the time they were winning nine championships in a row, so we thought we're in for a hammering here but we'll try to keep the score down as much as possible.'

But there is a sense of determination. Lou Macari's words have put fire in Thistle bellies and focused minds. If they were to go down then those in red and yellow would go down fighting.

'That Celtic team on paper was a fantastic team,' said Jimmy Bone. 'A real top-class side. But I don't know if it was my opinion, or if what Davie said rubbed off, but it was a huge factor Billy not playing.

'He was just everything in terms of organisation, being the leader, him not playing – and I think it was a last-minute thing – would disrupt Celtic, they won't be able to go and work on anything. Big Billy was also a huge factor in set pieces. Taking away that threat to your goal but also it gives you an opportunity to be a threat from your set pieces.'

'McParland's major message to us was to give it a go,' McQuade said. 'To go for them, and we did, and I think that is why we were successful because we did run at them.

'You look at their team and the quality was from the midfield forward. At the back you had a dodgy goalkeeper, Brogan was a very committed guy but not the most mobile, Tommy Gemmell was a wonderful player but they had George

Connelly who could be quite quixotic – some days he was brilliant some days he was hopeless and that day he did not play that well. Celtic were having to adjust to having no Billy McNeill telling them what to do.

'I don't even recall it [McNeill's absence] being mentioned before the game but we would have found out just ahead of kick-off. It was obvious that what Celtic lacked was a bit of leadership on the day and we took advantage of it.'

'I asked Billy after why he wasn't playing and he never gave me a definitive answer,' Rough added. 'Jock decided he just wasn't playing which was a strange one. But the main man was wee Jinky. Everything revolved around Jinky and, when I say this I don't mean it in the wrong way, but somebody had to "sort him oot". Somebody make sure he knows he's in a game.'

'Marching out I just wanted the game to start as soon as possible,' Bone said. 'You just want to go and get on with. It was great because it was a big crowd, I'd never played in a game with that size of crowd.

'Hand on heart we didn't think we could win. We thought we could cause them problems, we thought we would be in the game but the chances of winning were very slim.'

'Everybody had written us off and this is what gives you more of an incentive,' said Alex Forsyth. 'We never thought we would win. Of course, you're looking to put in a good performance but I was quietly confident that we had the players to go and score against anybody.

'Jimmy Bone and Frank Coulston were two strong, pacy players. We had two great wingers, Denis [McQuade] could beat anybody and wee Bobby [Lawrie] was a great winger and the midfield were so strong. We had a lot of energy in our team, we were fit boys.

'When I looked at the Celtic team, especially their defence, I was quietly confident we would score. We were definitely going to score, then the only trouble was they would likely score more goals than us because you had Jimmy Johnstone, Kenny Dalglish, Lou Macari, Harry Hood and Davie Hay. These were absolutely fantastic players but I thought that maybe their defence was not the greatest so we will score one goal at least.

'The absence of Billy McNeill, it didn't really make that much of a difference. He was the stalwart at the heart of their defence, he was their top man and I felt that gave us even more of a chance because we had Denis McQuade on the right, Bobby Lawrie on the left who was a flying machine. We had two great centre-forwards who were strong and very pacy and that is why I felt we would score. We had myself and John Hansen going up and down. We were good at attacking and they weren't too clever at the back.

'I thought we had the players to trouble them. Maybe we caught them on a bad day but I thought they were kind of cocky and showed too much confidence thinking they will turn up against a middle of the road team, brush us aside and overcome us.'

Ronnie Glavin is like a coiled spring. He can't wait to get going, to get at this Celtic team who have written his Thistle side off. Up until just two days before kick-off Glavin didn't know if he would play in the game at all. The ankle was still giving him problems but it was not going to stop him. Nothing was. He had faith in his body that it wouldn't let him down. He had faith in himself and his own ability. But above all he had total faith in the players alongside him. He may have been a Celtic supporter but this was his Thistle team.

'We were so fired up it wasn't true,' Glavin said. 'We had a way of playing. The one thing we had was that we had lads who could run. We had John Hansen at right-back, now you are talking about a right-back who could run up and down all day. Various players were good at various distances but John was a great 200m man and I knew that if I picked the ball up and John started his run I knew I just had to drop one in there for him. Then he's piling down there with power and pace to die for.

'Then we had Alex Forsyth who had an engine that was supercharged so we had two attacking full-backs who could bomb up and down there all day. You talk about today's game but that was what it was like.

'Then we had Frank Coulston. Now Frank didn't run, Frank could fly. And you had Jimmy [Bone] who was also quick, we had a bit of pace. Then you had [Bobby] Lawrie on the left wing who was a flying machine – I think he made his name chasing rabbits. We had pace in our team. Everything was right and if we could get going with the space at Hampden, knocking in behind with Frank and Jimmy on their bikes they were a real handful, we could give teams a game.'

And what of his partner in the engine room, the man helping him control the orchestra and make the machine tick?

'Alex Rae was a great midfield player,' said Glavin. 'In today's game Alex would have more of a holding role. He was experienced, did the sensible thing played the right ball and was tough and hard. He was an excellent, first-class player. Alex was tops.'

Rae, a ball in his hands, leads his team down the steps. He puffs out his chest.

'I'm a Govan boy, a lot of my pals were Rangers supporters, I was one of them too,' he said. 'It dawned on me about a week or a fortnight before it that I couldn't believe I was having the opportunity to put my ability against my youthful enemy if you wish. I was so focused on the task in hand.

'Just coming out the tunnel, the look on my face. You would have thought someone has stolen my favourite sweeties or something. I couldn't believe it was as stern looking as it was. I really felt we had a good set of boys, really good youngsters and if we performed as we could, because we were capable of playing really good football with serious attacking options, I really felt we had a serious chance although we were written off in numerous quarters.

'The build-up was really professional and it was something that made me feel we had an opportunity not to be missed.'

The noise is glorious now, both sets of fans welcoming their heroes. Let battle commence. History beckons.

* * *

'And here at Hampden Park it's going to be Celtic kicking off in the final of the Scottish League Cup.' – Arthur Montford's TV commentary

There are 62,470 people inside the national stadium. The rain that had fallen heavily ahead of the game has gone now but the surface is wet and when the kick-off is played long from Davie Hay it skids off the surface and behind to offer Alan Rough an early touch of the ball. Understandably, the vast number of press photographers are assembled around Rough's goal. The opening minutes are a time for the teams to size each other up, to look their opposite number in the eye and wonder, 'Are you on it today, son?' Thistle's players have taken McParland's instructions on board from the off and are harrying, pressing and biting into every tackle. A long ball down the Thistle right has the Celtic defence in trouble; Brogan is back-pedalling and unsure. A sign of nerves perhaps? He is pounced upon by the combined forces of Bone and Coulston, niggling, charging, never giving the Celtic defender a moment to settle. The ball is laid off to McQuade, who is ambling on to the scene in that laconic style of his, and as it breaks to him he sends a powerful effort narrowly wide of the right-hand post with Celtic goalkeeper Evan Williams diving nervously along his line. It is an early statement of intent, a shot across the Celtic bows.

'When you are playing a better team my theory is that when you are in that situation you are likely to get beat but have a go anyway,' McQuade said. 'Don't just wait and see if you can survive, wait until ten minutes to go and then have a go. Nine times out of ten they will crucify you. Have a go!'

Only six minutes have been played and Thistle's positive start has rattled the favourites. Celtic are not allowed to get into any rhythm and are unable to string their passes together. Even Jinky is feeling it. He is pounced upon in the middle of the park by Ronnie Glavin who steals the ball and begins to make ground. Glavin's influence on the encounter would be immense.

The Celtic defence is back-pedalling now and a clever one-two with Bone gives Glavin a sight of goal only for Davie Hay to nick the ball from his toe and send it out for a corner, just as Thistle's powerful midfielder was readying himself to shoot. McQuade fires it in and Bone is first to rise, his leap sending the ball towards the Celtic goal. There is panic in the Celtic defence, a first clearance is sent skyward, Tommy Gemmell's header only reaching the edge of the box. Alex Rae is lurking.

One swing of his right boot and the ball is arcing towards goal. It is placed, a thing of beauty. The players in the penalty box turn, watching as the ball arrows perfectly into the net. Williams does not even make an attempt.

'It's a goal! Rae scores for Thistle! Exactly ten minutes, Ronnie Glavin's tenacity won the corner, McQuade's corner wasn't properly cleared and Rae astutely lobbed the ball in under the corner of the crossbar and the post. What a dream start for Thistle!' exclaims Montford.

'Big Denis [McQuade] put the corner in and as always I would hover anywhere from the 18-yard box to maybe a wee bit deeper away from the goal,' said Rae. 'So that is exactly what I did. You are moving, readjusting, wee movements that there is no particular reason for. I'm watching Denis and when he starts his run I had gone forward, checked back and forward again and the timing was perfect. The ball reached into the box and came out and the rest is history. It was a well-struck attempt at goal.'

Rae's reaction after the passing of the years is understated but the memory of that moment remains crystal clear. Asked what it was like when the ball hit the back of the net, he laughs. That feeling came long before the ball crossed the line. In truth it was in the second the ball left his boot.

And that feeling of scoring the opener in a cup final?

'There is a tension, ooft, this could…and then it explodes,' he said. 'What I need to say is that after the goal went in and the guys are celebrating my biggest concern was, "It's only 1-0, it's Celtic, we need to batten down the hatches and stop the celebrating. It's too early to celebrate."

'You could take me through all four goals and after each goal I would still say what I felt at the time, how many times have Celtic come back when they are down? Maybe they've not been four down too often but if we can get four goals in the first half they could get five in the second. That was exactly my mentality. Celebrations happen when it is done, not when it is partially done.'

'He placed it,' said McQuade. 'It wasn't just a hopeful lob. He placed it.'

'Look at that goal, watch it back,' said Alex Forsyth. 'He did brilliantly because he had to take a couple of steps back. And then he volleyed in. A great goal. I just remember thinking, "Well, that's a good start anyway."'

Ronnie Glavin was marvelling at the quality of his midfield partner's finish.

'It was just fantastic,' he said. 'It dropped to him on the edge of the box and he took a half-volley, he just did what we would do at training. I think the goalkeeper appeared to be unsighted and you think, "Whoa! This gives us a chance!" We started believing then.'

Celtic start the game once again. It is noteworthy just how determined Thistle players are in winning the ball back. First Rae, then McQuade, then Glavin. Jinky Johnstone is penalised for snapping at Glavin and the Thistle midfielder picks up the ball and presents it to Johnstone's face. He's making a statement. 'Is this what you want? Is this what you want?' The ball is played down the right again where McQuade picks out Jimmy Bone. He is under pressure but he has his head up and his eyes pick out acres of space on the left where that pocket dynamo of a flying machine Bobby Lawrie is waiting, loitering with intent. Bone's right-foot pass is inch perfect. Lawrie kills the ball with his first touch. He is immediately in control, Hay is back-pedalling. Lawrie, a crackling box of tricks, feints to go left. For a split-second Hay is fooled as the Thistle man cuts back in on his right. The clock ticks into the 15th minute.

'Lawrie, edge of the box, inside, right-foot shot to the far side, and it's there! Lawrie scores a sensational goal. And look at those jubilant Thistle players,' says Montford on commentary.

Two goals in just five minutes and each one something special. No sclaffs off a defender's backside or a deflected speculative effort. It is real quality. The Thistle players mob Lawrie, and their Celtic counterparts are a picture of confusion. What the hell is going on?

'It was a brilliant feeling,' said Lawrie. 'I didn't score many goals so it was quite an achievement for me.

'Jimmy Bone gave me the ball on the left wing just outside the 18-yard box and I went to go round the outside and changed it to cut in on the inside with my right foot and swerved one right into the far corner.'

Celtic goalkeeper Williams had been left grasping at air. The green and white defence has been breached easily once again.

'I thought, "They're not good at the back, we have a wee chance here,"' said Alex Forsyth.

Celtic do indeed have real problems at the back and the absence of the influential McNeill is crystal clear. Even a 15-year-old in the stand can see it.

'Celtic had major problems down the centre of the defence,' said Alan Hansen. 'There were wide gaps everywhere.'

'They were shaken,' said Denis McQuade. 'And the more shaken they became the more spaces appeared. When you have got the perfect storm, with Bobby Lawrie on fire and the pace he had, he caused them untold problems down that left wing.

'Our tails were up. We're just saying, "Keep going, keep this going; they're not liking this." We just kept attacking rather than playing tippy-tappy round the middle, holding on to possession. You can't take time on the ball. We just decided to keep attacking.'

It is often the case that people who achieve great things are reliably understated in their recollections of them. What the supporter, the viewer, the audience see as moments of brilliance are just par for the course for the instigator. Such is the case with Lawrie and his goal. In fact, Lawrie would go on to turn in a man-of-the-match performance, an accolade he shrugs off with indifference. That does not mean such heroes go unappreciated. Not by the fans and certainly not by the players around them.

'He was one of the best wingers in Scotland, a smashing player,' Alex Forsyth said of Lawrie. 'Playing alongside wee Bobby, he was one of the fastest wingers in Scotland then, he had two good feet and he would just take the ball away. He had everything, a good attitude, he would take people on and come back and help you and he just dooked inside and hit it with his right. After his goal I thought "we can do this". That was the start of it.'

The boys at the back have hardly had anything to do, surprisingly untroubled despite the power and talent in the Celtic forward areas. Alan Rough is a virtual spectator. Experienced duo Hugh Strachan and Jackie Campbell marvel at what is unfolding in front on them. At least John Hansen and Alex Forsyth have been involved but only in forward areas. Everything is positive.

'It was unbelievable what was what was going through my head,' said Campbell. 'A team that had got it in their mind that they are going to win the game and start lazily, well it is very difficult to turn it around and get back into it.

'It was just knowing that we were two up and talking to the boys round about you. "Right, this is going to be our day, keep the pressure on." We knew we had to do what we had to do. We were on top of our game.'

Jimmy Bone is in confident mood also. He has had a hand in both goals and knows that Celtic will have to do something special to come back at Thistle.

'We've got them here,' he is thinking. 'Just keep it up.' All of a sudden that night shift and the darkness of the coalmine is light years away. The atmosphere is electric. Thistle's thousands of fans are in dreamland.

'We had pace in our team and if you underestimate it you are in trouble,' said Ronnie Glavin. 'We played balls behind Celtic and they could not cope with that.'

Celtic restart and must somehow find a foothold in a game that is already getting away from them. It is time for their big players to stand up. Jimmy Johnstone takes the ball from kick-off and begins his twists and turns. Glavin flies into one tackle and misses, McQuade goes into another and he too loses out. Johnstone has his head up now, attacking and foraging into space. Wide on the left, he is going up through the gears as Glavin appears on the scene once again. Bang! Thistle boot and Celtic knee collide.

'A bad tackle by Glavin,' says Montford in commentary.

Johnstone does not initially go down. Instead, he turns to confront his assailant. Tommy Gemmell joins the fray and referee Bill Mullan calms the situation. It is then that Johnstone looks down at his right leg and notices the gash, the blood slowly trickling out of the wound. He falls to the floor, his leg in the air.

'It wasn't meant, it was unfortunate but it turned out to be one of the best unfortunate things that ever happened to me,' said Glavin. 'I don't mean that nastily. Wee Jimmy, he would go one way, then the other way and he'll catch people out and he did that to me and I just happened to catch him.

'I was a person that if ever anybody said anything to me it got me going and as soon as that incident happened I said, "Jimmy I didn't mean to do that to you," and he called me for everything. I got threats from their players and all it did was rile me up. I wasn't going to take a back seat for that. I hated them, I wanted to win that game. I was a big Celtic fan but it meant nothing to me, it made no difference. Partick Thistle was my team.'

Mullan warns Glavin that one more like that and he would be in trouble. The modern-day player would have seen a card but this is 1971. Anything goes.

Johnstone limps round the red blaes perimeter, helped by physio Neilly Mochan. He is suffering badly. The deep gash will no doubt require a needle and thread.

Murdoch arrows the resulting free kick into the box. At last Rough is called into action, leaping high above Harry Hood to punch the ball clear. It breaks to Glavin and his rangy stride takes him clear. He tries to pick out Lawrie but Hay intercepts and finds Murdoch.

Celtic are still down to ten players but they are finding spaces and when they make their way into the Thistle box, only a perfectly timed Campbell tackle keeps them at bay.

'Jackie Campbell was the most underrated player in Scotland at that time,' said Alex Forsyth. 'He was absolutely magnificent but he never got the plaudits he should have got, because he was different class.'

From the Celtic bench there is activity. Substitute Jim Craig is removing his tracksuit and loosening up. Jimmy Johnstone's game is over, the leg gash too serious for him to return.

'I thought my big moment had come and I was going on at outside-right,' said Jim Craig. 'But we did a reshuffle and I ended up in my usual position.

'There were no fancy instructions from the manager. He just said get on with it. We all knew what we had to do. When you're 2-0 down you have got to come back pretty quickly otherwise it gives the other team more and more confidence as half-time approaches and sets them up for the second half.

'It was important that we tried to get back into the game.'

The task facing them has just got even harder. Watching on, Alex Forsyth is breathing a sigh of relief.

'The thing is that wee Jimmy played wide right, in the middle, he had a sort of roaming commission,' he said. 'A few of us gave him a few hard tackles as you would say, a couple of dull ones. He was the main man and if we could keep him quiet, we had a chance.

'When he went off injured I thought "well, we are in here".'

The feeling is shared by Jimmy Bone. 'The amount of times we played against Celtic and Jimmy used to tear us to bits,' he said. 'When Jimmy Johnstone was on song, he was unplayable. It gave us a second wind when wee Jimmy went off. That is another thing in our favour – it was the same feeling as if we had scored another goal, it galvanised us that much.'

'I wasn't disappointed seeing him go off,' said captain Alex Rae. 'Jim Craig came on and I didn't think him coming on for Jimmy Johnstone was going to improve Celtic. Wee Jimmy got knocked about a bit but he nearly broke my leg in a previous encounter at Firhill.'

'I had six years of playing against Jinky,' said Jackie Campbell. 'We all understood what he was like and what he was capable of. He was something else, this was Jinky Johnstone.

'Sometimes he overdid it. He would beat you and come back to beat you again and always give you a chance to get another tackle in. He was that type of player, jinked inside and outside but you always needed to get close to him to make it difficult for him to get control and come past you.

'We hadn't a fear of him because Alex [Forsyth] who was up against him was fast and could turn. And we weren't playing man for man, we were playing areas. As soon as we were savvy enough to know that we had the opportunity to go and make the tackle and hope you would win the ball, somebody was always covering for you so I don't remember us having any fear of him or even relaxing because he was away and off.

'What I do remember is getting thumped by Bobby Murdoch. He did me in the first half and I was out for about four or five minutes. That really riled me because it was one of these things where the ball is coming out from their goalkeeper and my feet were off the ground. I could see him coming, I was up for the ball and I got his elbow right across my jaw. I thought I'd broken it that day. Once you get back on your feet again, I could have been off, it was bad enough to knock me out but not bad enough for me to go off. I suffered for weeks after it with a sore jaw.'

Jock Stein is forced to regroup. The master tactician is rarely in this position, on the back foot and chasing a game everyone had confidently predicted would fall in his favour. Jim Craig is on and Hay pushed further forward.

From a Tommy Callaghan cross John Hansen heads clear but it falls only as far as Tommy Gemmell. As it hangs in the air, the Celtic defender readies his howitzer. Boom! Hansen meets it full in the face.

'That is stopped by John Hansen, who is right out the game,' says Montford.

Campbell and Forsyth are agents of concern as they stand over their poleaxed team-mate.

'That was actually good ball control, because I killed the ball dead,' said Hansen. 'Tommy just had such a phenomenal shot, if you look back and think what is happening now [with head injuries], physio Willie Ross just came on and rubbed my face and got me back up. There was no question of going off with concussion.'

There appears no question either of referee Mullan stopping the game. Campbell looks up to see Celtic are on the attack. Hansen will have to wait.

Only 25 minutes have transpired and there have already been enough incidents to grace any cup final. Slowly but surely news of Thistle's exploits is travelling far from Hampden and to places like Ibrox, where Rangers are playing Motherwell, to Cappielow where Morton are playing Aberdeen. There is a full fixture card in Scotland this day. And at each ground an ear is being turned to what is happening at the national stadium.

Lou Macari plays a loose ball inside which is gathered up by the flawless Campbell. His rangy stride takes him away from trouble and he picks out a perfect pass for Frank Coulston on the left. With pace to burn he outstrips the Celtic defence who, although in good number, seem to panic. Jim Brogan is spooked into conceding the corner.

'Lawrie with the corner. Up go the heads, chance for Thistle and McQuade scores. Sensation! Thirty minutes played and it's 3-0.' Montford's commentary tells the story.

'It's like ecstasy,' McQuade said. 'A bit of real elation, disbelief, excitement and it was only 30 minutes into the game. We're 3-0 up against Celtic in a cup final. It was fantastic.

'Both Jimmy [Bone] and I go up for the same ball, I think with Brogan and Connelly, Jimmy got to the ball and headed it.'

The ball is stopped on the line by a mangle of bodies, including Frank Coulston, but it breaks kindly for the Thistle winger.

'The ball just presented in front of me and I just tried to bundle it into the net as fast as possible,' McQuade said. 'I think it hit off Brogan's leg or back on the way in. It was just a matter of reacting to the ball being available and just getting it in the net. Of course, their goalkeeper is practically lying on the ground at this point, Brogan's on the ground so it was just one of these opportunistic situations that come your way.'

The Thistle celebrations are ecstatic. Just 28 minutes and the game is as good as won. Or is it?

'We were up for the challenge,' said Glavin, whose ankle is holding up, just. 'I always remember someone saying to me "if you treat the game easy it becomes hard, if you treat the game hard it becomes easy" and I think it was a case of us treating the game really hard. I won't say it was easy, it was relatively easy, but from Celtic's point of view I don't think they approached it in the same was as we did and it became hard for them.'

But this hadn't been in the plan. Even the tactically astute McParland couldn't have imagined this. An air of stunned disbelief hangs in the Hampden air. Is this really happening? How does a team cope in this situation? It's simple. Keep going. Don't change anything. Keep on the front foot. Attack, attack, attack.

'Davie's message was don't change anything for anybody,' said Frank Coulston. 'He would never say to Jimmy [Bone] or myself "come back and do a wee bit more defending". We were always thinking of going forward and so were the wide guys Dennis [McQuade] and Bobby Lawrie. The wide guys went up and down and that left Jimmy and me to cover the width of the pitch really but we were fit.

'We continued to play as we always played and, in some ways, attack was the best form of defence.'

Thistle continue to turn the screw. Minutes after their lead has been extended, Alex Forsyth plays the perfect pass to Jimmy Bone from deep in his own half.

'Alex Forsyth on the left side was a fantastic full-back, he went to Manchester United afterwards,' said Denis McQuade. 'He could ping a 60-yard ball to your toe without even looking up.'

Bone is twisting the Celtic defence. He lays it back to Bobby Lawrie who sees Denis McQuade in splendid isolation on the penalty spot. His shot is blocked as is Bone's effort with the rebound.

Montford's commentary is priceless, his voice soaring up a few octaves at the drama unfolding.

'Fantastic business going on in the goalmouth here,' he bellows. 'What a sensation!'

Thistle lead by three but it could be four, perhaps even five. An effort from Tommy Callaghan warms Rough's hands but it is routine stuff. His long clearance carries into the centre circle where Bone lurks. The interchange between the front pairing of Bone and Coulston is causing all sorts of problems, the latter forcing Gemmell into conceding a free kick.

Glavin's ankle is giving him concern and he has limped over the byeline to receive treatment from Willie Ross. Bobby Lawrie has wandered over from the opposite side of the pitch to take the free kick wide on the right.

'Celtic marshalling their forces. Taken by Lawrie – in comes Bone, he walks the ball into the net. It's four nothing!' The words from Montford are almost impossible to take in.

The Celtic defenders have gone to sleep as the ball is flighted in. Shellshocked, they seem happy to leave it to somebody else, anybody else. They are statues while Bone is a ball of activity, alive and ready.

'It was a free kick but for some reason the Celtic defenders were very, very high,' said Bone. 'When the ball is about to be played in, I just did a thing which we had worked on often. We used to change direction, change pace to get in behind the defender. When I went for the ball I was actually aware of no one else being in sight. The goalkeeper stopped for some reason, he must have thought I was offside or something. It was just a case of going in and it came off the sole of my boot. It was quite bizarre, quite strange and certainly not the type of goal Celtic were used to losing.'

'It was surreal,' said Denis McQuade. 'Again, we're on the attack, get the free kick and they are all leaving it to each other. This was part of the inexperience of the Celtic defence. Billy McNeill would never have allowed that to happen, he would have attacked the ball but I think between Brogan and Connolly, they left it to each other. They left it to each other and Jimmy just ran in between them and trapped it effectively and walked it into the net.'

Hampden is now in a state of shock.

'It was utter disbelief, this can't be really happening,' said McQuade. 'Four-nil up and that carried through into half-time. The first half was just a blur but if they looked at possession and where the game was played, we would be 70 per cent in their part of the pitch in that first half. We just never stopped attacking them and they were not finding it easy to get out.'

McQuade is one of the few players to congratulate Bone. Glavin, by now back to his feet and walking back to the halfway line, barely acknowledges his team-mate or what he has done. The disbelief that envelops those in the stand and terracing has carried on to the pitch and into the heads of the players.

'You couldn't believe it,' said Glavin. 'I could hardly walk. Oh, my goodness, I do recall that. Everything was surreal at the time, a strange situation. And from Celtic's point of view, I'm sure that they were unsure what had happened to them and they were desperate to get in so that Jock Stein can sort it out for them. It was like, we've won this half, this half is over. It was a case of let's get ourselves together.'

'The celebrations were muted,' Bone said. 'I wanted the referee to blow the whistle and get off the pitch. My thinking was that the last thing we need is for Celtic to score before half-time because they would get a boost from that.

'Celtic, sometimes when we played them, could go on a run and score three goals. Bang! Bang! Bang! And that team was capable of going and doing that so my thought after the goal was blow for half-time because let's get in. Let's get regrouped.'

On the bench, substitute Johnny Gibson has had a ringside seat watching events unfold. Of course, he was desperate to be out there and be part of it. It's not easy being the 12th man. But at least he is close to the action and a witness to how the manager and his coaches are reacting.

'It was a case of disbelief,' Gibson said. 'It was hard to get your head round one goal, two, three, four; is this really happening? It was difficult to take in, especially against that Celtic team. McParland didn't really say much. It was disbelief that the boys were taking Celtic apart.'

There would be eight long minutes before referee Mullan would call a halt to proceedings. When he did, the ecstatic, astonishing cheers from the Thistle fans carried through the air.

Montford desperately tries to sum up what he has just witnessed but you can tell in his voice the sense of disbelief.

'You can hear what the Thistle fans think of their team's fantastic performance,' he says.

'As memorable a first 45 minutes as Partick Thistle have ever played, anywhere against anybody.'

CHAPTER 9

THE INTERVAL

THISTLE'S players begin their journey back to the dressing room. A sanctuary away from the glorious madness they have experienced over the last 45 minutes. Initially they stroll but soon, to a man, they are jogging. Get inside. Let's hear what manager, team-mates and colleagues have to say.

'Right, lads. Deep breath. Calm yourselves down because now we go again,' will be the message.

There is a unity in their return. A team ethic, a team together. As they pick up the pace, they trot past Celtic players who look lost. Rudderless, and in no way inclined to rush back to a dressing room where a furious Jock Stein awaits their arrival.

Davie McParland has raced from the Thistle bench, up the tunnel and into the dressing room. He wants to be ready for his boys when they get in. This could be the biggest 15 minutes of his career, and all their careers. He must immediately judge the mood, calm those who exhibit signs of nerves and slap down those who think this game is won.

Soon he hears the sound of studs on the concrete as his players climb the steps. Click-clack-click. The door opens. In they come.

'The mood was surreal,' said Jackie Campbell. 'We couldn't believe we were 4-0 up. There was such a positivity.'

A tray of sandwiches, pots of tea and cups and saucers sit incongruously on a table in the dressing room. Who the hell wants tea and sandwiches at a time like this? They remain untouched. Outside, above the sound of 62,740 people, the band of the Royal Marines has struck up 'Scotland the Brave'.

McParland's stomach is doing somersaults but he must exude calm. In his wildest dreams he couldn't have imagined this. Four goals in under 40 minutes. But he knows exactly what he is going to tell his players – change nothing, do it all again.

In a television studio in London, Frank Bough is hosting *Grandstand* as the half-time scores come in.

'And in the League Cup Final in Glasgow, it's 4-0 Partick Thistle,' he says, before pausing. 'Hmmm, I'm not sure about that. We'll check it out for you, it might be a mistake.'

'We couldn't believe it. Nobody anywhere in the country could believe we were 4-0 up against a team like Celtic. Their defence was shocking that day,' said Alex Forsyth. 'What a chance, 4-0 up after 40 minutes and we are cruising. It could have been more. It's a fairytale.'

From the corner of his eye Alex Rae can see two of the team are not as focused as he would like.

'There was a lot of young guys in there and there were a couple of them going over the top so in my role as captain I had to have a word with them,' Rae said. 'Ronnie [Glavin], one of the best players I ever played with, and Alex Forsyth – they were celebrating prematurely as far as I was concerned. So, we had a wee chat and the message was there. They calmed down a wee bit.

'McParland had been speaking but this was almost aside, quietly I see the two of them doing wee dances, I don't want to sound like a disciplinarian because I'm not but there was a responsibility not just on the park but off the park in my role as captain. I was very proud to be captain of Partick Thistle and I wasn't going to let early celebrations result in a disaster for the club.'

But these are young players, kids even, and they are in dreamland. The trick is to keep them grounded. Jimmy Bone recalled, 'Everybody was on a high, patting each other on the back, talking at the one time.'

McParland has let them take the first few moments together to let off some steam. Now it is his turn. The most important half-time team talk of his life.

'Everyone sit down, quiet,' McParland says. 'Calm down.'

'We didn't say anything, it was Davie who always talked,' said Ronnie Glavin. 'We were just a group of young lads and when Davie talked, we listened. It was a case of just trying to keep calm. I do recall people were more agitated and there was more excitement within the group. Davie was trying to calm everyone down.'

'We have to put a shift in now,' McParland says. 'We need to be ready to work hard because this half is going to be different. Our mentality has to be right, we're going to have to graft. We're going to have to chase everything and run everything down.

'Just keep doing your jobs, the way you are doing now. Keep going. Keep passing it, keep holding it. Steady it up, don't defend, try to get forward.

'This isn't over, we all know what they are capable of.'

* * *

Across the corridor, no more than a few paces from where McParland is talking, the Celtic dressing room is filled with a different mood, a different kind of managerial address to the troops. Mere footsteps separate both sides. Yet it could be a world away.

The confidence that had been so apparent ahead of kick-off has gone. Jock Stein is looking around at his shattered and crestfallen team. Bitter recent experience had told him never to allow himself or his team to underestimate an opponent. But had he got it wrong? Could he, should he, have risked starting his rock at the back, Billy McNeill?

The players are silent – Jimmy Johnstone is sitting on the treatment table, the gash in his leg clear for all to see after having four stitches inserted into the wound. Young players Lou Macari, Davie Hay and Kenny Dalglish look dazed but even those who have been with Stein for years and tasted the glory of Lisbon know this is not their place to talk.

He is furious at the way his team have performed. And the defence is being singled out for special attention.

'We would have been listening to the boss,' said Jim Craig. 'And at half-time there was not much input from players because the boss was the boss. He was the man who controlled things. We believed in him and trusted him but you can imagine how he felt. He put out this team to win a League Cup Final and they are four down at half-time. Bloody hell. It must have been a shock to him as well.

'He was really annoyed at the situation we were in and drilling into us to get back out there and back into the game as quickly as possible, to change things around. "Do not let them control the play as they had done in the first half. We have to get back into this," he would have said. But we were probably a wee bit shellshocked ourselves and it took a wee while to recover.

'We were used to dominating games but on that day we were brought down to earth with a bump and suddenly we are under the cosh at this point. I could hear that the management team were taken aback by that as well, that Thistle had come out to take the game by the scruff of the neck and come right at us. And at the back we were taken to the cleaners.

'I am a great man when people ask, "What do you have to do to win a game?" I always say, well, that the players have to rise to the occasion. That is the first thing you have to do. All ten outfield players and the goalkeeper have to rise to the challenge. Every Thistle player rose to the challenge and possibly not everyone of us rose to the challenge if I am being honest.

'I don't think we underestimated Partick Thistle. Jock was not somebody to underestimate an opponent and that had been even more true after losing to Feyenoord in the [European Cup] final the season before because we had been accused of underestimating them. In a sense there was a wee element of that, and of course having beaten Leeds in the semi-final, that was regarded as a major achievement by all the press. Sometimes players can be affected by that in spite of being warned by managers, "Don't pay any attention to what they say, they're seeing it from a different angle." But if you're constantly getting praised for your performance it sometimes gets into your system without you thinking about it.

'We were kind of fired up for things but I've never seen a team as well prepared as Partick Thistle. From the very first minute they were firing on all cylinders.

'They raided down both flanks and raided through the middle. They were just raiding like nobody's business and were really fired up for it. They came at us like furies.

'I can't stress too highly how much they controlled the play. They were really dominant, and deserved a lot of credit for how their players rose to the occasion.

'On the day they were exceptional. Any team you name they would have given them a game on that day.'

For the men in green and white this is time to regroup. There are still 45 minutes to go. Unbeknown to them there are elements within the Thistle dressing room now fearing a Celtic whirlwind. A force of nature that says if Thistle can score four goals in the first half then Celtic, this Celtic team, transition or no transition, are more than capable of scoring five in the second. Sections of the Thistle support fear that too. The media, struggling to comprehend what they have just witnessed, expect normality to return when play resumes.

'The strange thing was that even at 4-0 there is a way back here,' said Davie Hay. 'There was huge disappointment when we went in at half-time. Every time Thistle went up the park they looked as if they would score. I mean, they were 4-0 up at half-time!

'We had to go out and try and improve. I think we thought possibly if we could get a quick enough goal it could be the start of it.

'We had to think that way but to be fair Thistle was a strong team defensively, they had decent players at the back. I don't think we underestimated Thistle. On reflection people may think that but Thistle to a man played exceptionally well, individually and collectively, they had a first-class manager in Davie McParland. We just didn't produce it.'

Stein's message is simple. Be better. Be what you know you can be. Attack Thistle from the first opportunity. There is hope. Nothing is lost yet.

Captain Alex Rae (No10) and Denis McQuade (No7) begin the celebrations as goal scorer Bobby Lawrie turns away after scoring the second goal.

Denis McQuade pounces on the loose ball after a corner and prepares to slam home for the third goal.

Jimmy Bone ghosts past a static Celtic defence to slot home the fourth goal.

Arms raised, Jimmy Bone is in dreamland as he celebrates his goal.

The cup-winning team, although curiously John Gibson is absent from this photograph.

BACK ROW: Davie McParland; Jackie Campbell; John Hansen; Alan Rough; Alex Forsyth; Ronnie Glavin, Hugh Strachan, Willie Ross.

FRONT ROW: Denis McQuade, Frank Coulston, Alex Rae, Jimmy Bone, Bobby Lawrie, Tommy Rae.

'You have always to believe you could get it back,' said Jim Craig. 'You can never think that the game has gone. You have always got to think that you can come out and do better.

'It was important that we tried to get back into the game. But it was very difficult and their management team had got them fired up for the occasion, did a great job with them and deserve the highest praise.

'We would have been chivving each other on a wee bit to make sure we were ready for the second half.'

'Come on Bhoys, we must do better!'

* * *

High above, in the press box which clings to the roof of the main stand, there is shock at what has been unfolding on the pitch below. From this vantage point journalists have an unfettered view of the action but many have been rubbing their eyes in disbelief.

Yet they had been warned.

'On their day, on their free-running, brave, very often daft game, Thistle are capable of beating any team in Scotland – including Celtic,' wrote Malcolm Munro on the eve of the game in the *Evening Times*.

'Thistle will win. Davie McParland has the right idea – he is coming at you from the front not the back,' said St Johnstone manager Willie Ormond.

In truth, however, nobody in the stunned-into-silence press box had given Thistle any chance at all. Now they were hastily rewriting intros, calls back to sports desks began with phrases like 'we need a rethink here'. Incredulous sports editors, unable to see pictures of the miracle unfolding, are demanding details of just what the hell is going on.

Slung below the press box, in an eyrie almost hanging from the stand roof, Archie Macpherson and Arthur Montford have been commentating for the BBC and STV respectively. They are somewhat removed and isolated from the newspaper pack above them, but they too are in shock.

'I went to Hampden that day thinking of it purely as a formality but it was like a mirage,' Macpherson said. 'It was stunning when you think back on it that this apparent Celtic juggernaut was being derailed very quickly.

'There was no co-commentator that day because it was not live, it was recorded highlights, so I wasn't quite sure how others were reacting to this. I was astonished.

'Celtic were without McNeill and maybe that had something to do with it. Celtic were simply rolled over. I think Lawrie was very important, the width of Thistle was hugely influential in that game. And also their attitude. I don't think they were overawed and that is very important when you played the Old Firm. I mean, Billy McNeill told me once when he had the Aberdeen team at Hampden to play Rangers he said they knew they were beaten as they walked into the stadium because in his dressing room they were all worried about playing Rangers whereas he had come from the Celtic tradition.

'With Thistle that day there was no apparent tension in their play. They swept the ball about and I know it might sound incredible to say this, but it looked as if they were enjoying it. And if you get that sense of enjoyment in your game, it doesn't matter who you're playing, you'll probably do well, you'll communicate well, so that the individual also becomes a team player and that showed up classically in that game.

'We were fairly isolated. We were in a platform slung under the press box and we had to climb down from the press box area to get to the commentary area so we were totally isolated. We were insulated from the press box. I imagine the press box was in chaos, with rewrites and rethinking going on that's for sure.

'But I had an affection for Thistle, as we all had, to get away from the hard nuts and so on and being at the BBC there were a lot of Thistle supporters because of the locality. Some of the famous actors were Thistle supporters.

'But they [Thistle] didn't stand out. And I am not the only one who would say that. I mean, I saw them, I did commentaries on them and they would go by and you would forget them until the next time they cropped up.

'We always liked going to Firhill to do a game so we had that kind of affection for them but I wasn't drilled very closely about their players.

'The sad thing about television, maybe not so bad now as it was then, we virtually did about three or four teams. We would do the Old Firm, Hibs and Hearts, Aberdeen, and of course we covered Thistle [but] it was incidentally that we covered Thistle. If they were playing against the Old Firm, or against Hearts. In other words they were the props for some of the games.

'And that is why when we got to that final I'm sure mentally we had dismissed them before we got there. They were the accompanying act for other victors.

'They were always the perpetual also-rans in our minds and in that respect when we got to Hampden that day there was not a soul outside of the Thistle camp itself who thought they had the slightest chance.'

So, there is a feeling among the press boys that reality will return. That Stein would work his magic in the dressing room at half-time and Celtic would emerge a different animal for the second half. Could Stein turn it around?

'Well yes, in a word. He seemed invincible,' said Macpherson. 'He seemed the kind of man who would be able to go in and change something. We couldn't believe, I mean, I don't think 4-0 down that we ever thought Celtic were beaten at half-time. Because I had seen them come through so many victories and so many late victories as well.

'Dating from when they won the cup against Dunfermline [in 1965], Billy McNeill's header and so on, there was that feeling "no they're going to come back" because the whole thing was just unbelievable; 4-0 up [yet] there was that feeling Celtic will come back in this. That sensation I am sure was universal in the press box as well.'

* * *

It is half-time too across Glasgow at Ibrox and the natives are not happy. Motherwell are the visitors and with the game goalless at the interval the Rangers players have just been booed off the park.

Then, amid the chatter of complaint, the Ibrox announcer reads out the score from Hampden. For two, perhaps three, seconds there is silence as the reality dawns. Then there is a cheer of such intensity it is as if Rangers have scored. Fans begin dancing in the terracing, their unhappiness at their side's first-half performance forgotten. Others begin heading for the exit, desperately looking to flag down a taxi and head for Hampden. The number of Thistle supporters at the national stadium is about to swell.

The Thistle fans have cheered themselves hoarse over the first 45 minutes. In the stand Robert Reid turns to his father.

'I said to him hesitantly, "Do you think we can win this game?" and of course he said I was to stop being silly. But there were still 45 minutes. Such was my lack of confidence that I had a terrible feeling we would lose 5-4.'

Not far away from Reid, a young Alan Hansen can't believe what he has witnessed. Alongside his father and his uncle, they are struggling to take it all in. If this is a dream then they don't care to be awoken.

'Everybody was shellshocked,' he said. 'It was like an out-of-body experience. It was like it hadn't happened, that this was not it, but I suppose if there was one team that could ever do it, it was Thistle. That was what Thistle were all about really.

'It's 4-0 but the question is can you hang on? The longer the game went, there was no way Celtic were going to score four. Celtic had major problems down the centre of the defence and there were just wide gaps everywhere. Thistle exploited that in the first half and it was like, it wasn't cruise control because you are up against Celtic, but if the score had been 2-0 maybe even 3-0 then you would have been nervous and thinking you know what's coming.'

Further along the main stand, Terry McParland is part of the official Thistle party, surrounded by like-minded people who have spent 40 minutes of the opening period in stunned celebration of what they were witnessing. The first goal had been great, the second wonderful but the third and fourth? There is a sense of shock.

As she rises to her feet to make her way downstairs for a cup of tea, Scot Symon reaches across to her.

'That's your husband won the cup,' he says.

'My mum was thinking "no way, there's still the second half to come",' said daughter Yvonne. 'She was not counting on anything, she wasn't counting that we wouldn't win, she just thought, "This is Celtic, they could come back in the second half and score five goals." Which would have been awful.'

Back in Roselea Drive the McParland girls are blissfully unaware of what is happening.

'The three of us were at home, Aunty Vera was watching us and we were just outside playing and not listening on the radio,' said Yvonne. 'The manageress of the pub that my mum and dad owned had phoned my aunt to say, "I don't know if you're listening to the radio but it's 4-0."'

Vera asks the caller to hold on. 'Let me get Yvonne,' she says.

'I came in and the lady, Betty, said "listen hen, it's 4-0". My words were "my poor dad" and she said, "No, it's not for Celtic, it's 4-0 for Thistle," at which point I don't think I believed her either. It was great.'

* * *

McParland looks around the dressing room, it is time for some individual instruction, and some quiet words of wisdom. He spots his strike pairing of Jimmy Bone and Frank Coulston.

'He came and spoke to myself and Frank and said it was really important that we give a length to the game so that if we get it, we can play it,' said Bone. 'He told us that we had to turn any ball into a good ball.'

The guys at the back are going to be key too. They must be ready for the onslaught.

'All the time even when you were 4-0 up, we still thought we were going to get beat because this was Celtic we're playing and they'll work out how to overcome us,' said John Hansen. 'They'll be in their dressing room and Stein will be going off his head. He'll have worked out how to overcome this non-stop attack and we'll get beat 5-4.

'People say to me there was no fear but that was just the way McParland had drummed into us for months before that this was how we were going to play and attack and sometimes we'll win, sometimes we won't.

'That was just the way they played. That was McParland's way. A 4-2-4 formation, the full-backs just attacked all the time, I mean, we didn't know any better. We just attacked and attacked.'

'I never thought we had won it at half-time,' said Alan Rough. 'I didn't think we would get beat 5-4 but I did think that they might score two or three because that is the way they were. Although we were an attacking team, they were definitely an attacking side and we knew in the second half they had to come to us.'

Alex Forsyth isn't worried. He has seen what happened in the first half and can't believe Celtic, even this Celtic, have it in them to come back. He knows that there is every chance they will score – but he has faith.

'I can't remember Alan Rough having a great save to make in the first 45 minutes, nothing that you wouldn't expect your goalie to save,' he said. 'He had nothing to do. With the forward line that they had, the problem was their defence, they couldn't defend. I thought that even if they did score, we had the players who could go up and score again.'

The clock is ticking now. The 15 minutes have flown by. It feels like seconds since the players arrived back in the dressing room and now McParland must send them out to do it all again.

Jackie Campbell and Hugh Strachan catch each other's eye. If there is to be an expected Celtic onslaught, a wave of green and white attack, then these defensive figureheads must be the rocks on which it perishes.

'We would need to defend better than we ever defended before because they would come at us,' Campbell said. 'But if we weathered that storm then we would make it very difficult for them to score five goals.

'You just have to keep belief in yourselves and go out and play the way you are playing and give it your all. It was just so positive in the dressing room, the team, we just had such a belief in ourselves.'

Ronnie Glavin has spent much of the half-time break fretting. Will his ankle hold up? He had needed treatment before the first half had finished, and had been off the field when Jimmy Bone knocked in the fourth. Will he last though? Will he have to?

Start the second period the way they had the first and there is no chance for Celtic. He recalls the wise words of coach and club legend Jackie Husband, 'The one thing you never do, never give a bum a chance!' and he knows what this wise owl of the Thistle backroom staff means. Even a fighter dead on his feet can throw a lucky punch and send you to the canvas.

'Celtic were more than capable of scoring that amount of goals against us,' Glavin said. 'They had such a good side, they had world-class players in their team. So, don't underestimate them, we knew that even at 4-0 at half-time Celtic were capable of that, make no mistake about it. They had enough quality in their side to do that. Credit goes to the guys at the back, Hugh Strachan, Jackie Campbell and Roughie were outstanding. So, we were fortunate, but our attitude was brilliant.'

* * *

The bell tolls again. It is time, gentlemen. The Thistle players rise as one, like paratroopers ready to exit a Dakota over Normandy.

Davie McParland is ready to send them on their way. His mouth is dry, the butterflies in his stomach remain but he knows he must give them a last few words of wisdom.

He must be the father figure so many of his team recognise him to be. History can hang heavy on a man's shoulders, so he must ease that burden.

As his players prepare to head out he turns to them. The sound of the Royal Marine band marching off to the tune of 'A Life on the Ocean Wave' carries into the dressing room as the door opens.

'We just need to close up shop for the first 15 minutes,' McParland says. 'If we get past that first 15 minutes without losing a goal we're home and dry. So, concentrate your efforts in not letting them back into the game.'

And with that they are off, Alex Rae at the front once again. Down the steps with a clatter of studs on concrete and back out into the Hampden air, where they are greeted not with rousing cheers from the Thistle support, but with the curious sound of silence.

CHAPTER 10

THE SECOND HALF

PERHAPS they had cheered themselves hoarse. Perhaps it was the shock of what they had witnessed in that glorious first half. Perhaps it was the fear of what may come next. Whatever the reason, as the Thistle players take to the field for the second period their fans are not in full voice. Far from it.

'There was an eerie atmosphere,' said Alan Rough, by now running towards the massed ranks of the Thistle support who would be behind his goal. He needed something other than silence. He had expected a rousing reception to help ease his nerves and something to reinforce a belief that they can do this.

'At the start of second half it was quiet,' said Alex Forsyth. 'Nobody could believe it. Even us, we couldn't believe it.'

Jimmy Bone is heading towards the centre spot. Referee Bill Mullan has placed the ball ready to get the second period under way.

'It was strange going out for the second half because you were actually thinking, "Jesus Christ! It's 4-0; is it 4-0?"' he said. 'You start to doubt what actually happened.

'It was very quiet when we ran on to the field. The Celtic fans weren't making much of a noise, the Thistle fans weren't making much of a noise, there wasn't anything from the players. It was actually quite strange.'

'When we went in [at half-time] our fans were going bananas, when we came back out they were comatose,' said John Hansen. 'I said to someone "our fans aren't making any noise" because before half-time they were very vocal.

'The first 30 minutes of the second half, all you could hear was the Celtic fans screaming and shouting and nothing coming from our fans because they thought Celtic are going to wake up and they're going to get at us.'

The experienced older heads in the Thistle ranks are unaware of the lack of noise coming from the fans. They are focused on the job in hand. Alex Rae, Jackie Campbell, Frank Coulston all know that Celtic will come at them, and that Jock Stein would have sent his side out demanding they attack from the first opportunity.

'We continued to play as we played and in some ways attack was the best form of defence,' said Coulston. 'We knew that Celtic would be angry and hurt at 4-0 so they would come at us. Everybody put their bodies on the line.'

'We couldn't believe we were 4-0 up but there was a positivity in what we were doing,' said Jackie Campbell. 'We would need to defend better than we ever defended before because they would come at us but if we weathered that storm then we would make it very difficult for them to score five goals.

'So, you just have to keep believing in yourselves and go out and play the way you are playing and give it your all. It was just so positive; the team just had such a belief in ourselves.'

'Davie just told us told to steady it up, don't defend, try and get forward and just keep doing what we had been doing,' said Bobby Lawrie. 'We knew Celtic were going to come hard at us. Which they did.'

Alex Rae is imploring his players to dig deep. If they need to, he tells his defenders, play it long. Don't take chances. Don't give them a sniff.

'We're four up,' he says. 'Just keep doing what you've been doing, the simple things, keep the ball. Simple passing. Working hard and getting goal side of your opponent.'

'If you were in trouble you knocked it up to Frank and Jimmy,' said Alex Forsyth. 'They could bring it down good in the air, good link-up players, ideal for the full-back if you are looking for a get-out target, knock it up the park and one of them would get on the end of it.

'The older heads kept us at it. They just said "keep your shape, don't get carried away, don't do anything stupid, they might score a goal or two", which I thought they would do anyway. They kept us together.'

'I knew the way we played there wasn't a thought of us saying "right, 4-0 up, let's fall in to five at the back and four in the middle and sit it out",' said Ronnie Glavin. 'We just got out and carried on where we left off. We were a very attacking side, we didn't really defend at all, if you look at some of the results we had you can see that. You just defended your box.

'Jackie and Hughie would attack everything that is in the air and John and Alex would be attacking full-backs.'

What Thistle have to do is send out a message as soon as the sound of Bill Mullan's whistle echoes into the Hampden air.

* * *

'So, Thistle kick-off at the start of the second half leading by four goals to nil. A tremendous first half in which they played really well.' – Arthur Montford

Frank Coulston and Jimmy Bone start the second half for Thistle. Within two passes the ball finds its way to Bobby Lawrie deep in his own half and wide out on the left.

Three Celtic players come at him but Lawrie is going up through the gears. They can't touch him. He plays the ball forward into space and he is off, tearing down the line like a sprinter. There is a clever dummy from Coulston who allows the ball to run clear through his legs into Lawrie's path. His head is up, his eyes seeking out targets and team-mates. He sees and finds Bone on the edge of the box and the striker's clever cut back is perfectly placed for the onrushing Denis McQuade. He is 30 yards from goal but one sweet sweep of his left peg and the ball is arrowing towards the top right-hand corner of Evan Williams's goal. Agonisingly it is inches too high and flies over the cross bar. But a message has been sent. It is loud and clear.

'That had a great positive effect on the team because we're winning 4-0 but we're still wanting to attack,' said Alex Rae. 'It barely skims the top of the bar.'

Thistle stay on the front foot, working hard in the Celtic half to keep possession and disrupt any chance of Celtic building an attack. The front pair are working like Trojans, harrying and closing down the Celtic rearguard. Don't give them a platform on which to create.

But Celtic are far too talented an opponent to keep in the corner for the whole of the contest. Like a prize fight, the underdog has controlled the centre of the ring. Now it is the turn of the champion. As the match ebbs and flows they come off the ropes, tentatively at first, flashing a jab here and there. But they are on the front foot. The centre of the ring is theirs now.

Tommy Gemmell starts an attack from deep in his own half, driving forward. Ronnie Glavin tries to get back at him but is trailing in the Celtic man's exhaust fumes. Gemmell can see huge, gaping holes in the Thistle defence. That crucial commodity of space unfolds in front of him. There must be 20 yards of clean air between Jackie Campbell and John Hansen, occupied by the green and white shirt of Kenny Dalglish.

Gemmell's through ball is perfect, allowing Dalglish to let it roll past him and he is in on goal. Alan Rough is on his six-yard box and advances to close the angle, diving and sprawling at Dalglish's bootlaces.

'It must be a goal,' says Arthur Montford.

From behind the goal, the silent Thistle support hold their breath. An early Celtic strike is what they feared. For them it is slow motion now.

Dalglish lifts the ball over the diving Rough but it is too high. And it is still rising at is flies over the crossbar.

The first sound of the Thistle fans in the second half is a roar of relief.

But it is a warning. The yellow wall has been breached far too easily – and Jackie Campbell and Hugh Strachan know it. They arrow in on Hansen. The young full-back had switched off, allowing Dalglish to ghost past him. Don't let it happen again.

'A glorious chance for Celtic,' says Montford. 'But Thistle still lead four nothing.'

In the dugouts both managers remain impassive. But they know how important these chances can be. McParland is aware of just what a let off it has been. Stein is acutely aware that all chances must be taken, particularly that one had been gilt-edged.

The key to the game now is the middle of the park. This is where it will be won or lost.

'We have to put a shift in now,' Glavin thinks to himself. 'We need to be ready to work hard because this half is going to be different. We are going to have to graft. We're going to have to chase everything and run everything down.'

But the game is being played in the Thistle half. While they have chances of their own, much of their work and energy is being spent running towards their own box. And from behind the goal, the fans remain silent.

Rough is called on to deal with a Tommy Callaghan shot. The young goalkeeper had little to do in the first half but he has his work cut out now.

And still the clock ticks. Thistle fans looking at watches are convinced the hands are moving slower now. But the minutes tick by: 68, 69, 70.

Jim Craig finds possession on the right, midway inside the Thistle half. He has time to pick out a Celtic player with his cross and Lou Macari wins it, knocking it down into space in the Thistle box. Hansen is under pressure and the ball bounces high, adding to his woes, as he only succeeds in playing it back into the path of the Celtic man.

'Here's a chance for Macari now. Out in front, it must be a goal. Dalglish scores. Twenty-five minutes gone in the second half and certainly no more than Celtic deserve. They've been hammering away since the second half started,' says Montford as Celtic get one back.

The goal is far from pretty. A speculative cross, a sclaffed clearance, a melee in the six-yard box, before Macari rolls the ball under Rough where Dalglish is waiting for a tap-in. Hansen is distraught.

'It was my fault, the goal,' he said. 'I tried to clear it and it bounced quite high and I went to kick it and it hit my knee. I was feeling really bad but the boys never said anything. We got back on with it.

Even then I'm still thinking they are going to win.'

As the Thistle players walk back to the centre circle, very little is said. There is no rousing battle cry from Alex Rae; no raised fists of determination.

'When Kenny scored the goal it was unfortunate but I didn't feel that it was a killer blow in anyway,' he said. 'We just regrouped.'

Thistle are instead workmanlike, as if to say 'okay, it's a setback, but we go again'.

Alex Forsyth remains confident but there is a crumb of concern.

'I hope they don't get the next one quick,' he thinks. 'If they score again quickly we could be in a wee bit of a problem.'

'I wasn't worried,' said Jackie Campbell. 'We were never concerned about it, well I certainly wasn't. I never thought that they would score five goals against us. One because we had a good defence and two because you had Roughie at your back.'

'You're trying to keep focused,' said Glavin. 'Do what you are good at doing and keep plugging away. Everybody just kept going, we knew at some stage that they would cause us a problem or two because they were Celtic – a great team.'

Tellingly, as the game prepares to restart there is no great battle cry from the men in green and white. Are they resigned to their fate?

'Although the Celtic players were going and trying really hard you could see it in their faces that they didn't believe,' said Bone. 'They were gone, they were trying everything but you could see it in their faces.'

'We're 25 minutes in [to the second half] when we get one back and even one goal is not going to help when you are four down,' said Jim Craig. 'I I think we had the chance to score another goal or two but we were realistic at the same time.'

Back in Milngavie, three girls have just been called in from playing by Aunty Vera. 'We got called in to listen on the radio, in fact she switched it on just as Kenny Dalglish scored his goal,' said McParland's daughter Yvonne.

On the Thistle bench, McParland is in conversation with Jackie Husband. He has a plan. There are 20 minutes to go, in which Celtic will try to turn the screw. But they can do nothing, they cannot hurt his team if they do not have the ball.

He turns to where Johnny Gibson is seated and tells him to get ready.

There is still time for Bobby Lawrie to bring out the best in Evan Williams with a long-range effort which he touches past the post. And still time for Rough to brilliantly repel a Macari header.

But Glavin's ankle is bothering him again, so Gibson is stripped and ready for action. All the frustration at missing out in a place from the start, at his decision to stand aside for the Falkirk semi-final, can now be taken out on Celtic for these last 15 minutes.

'The only time Davie mentioned anything to me was just before I was going on,' Gibson said. 'He said, "Go on, hold the ball up and take it for a walk. Do your thing." I knew what I was capable of. It was just Davie's way of saying do your thing and the game will be over. Which was true. The longer we were keeping the ball the more the time was being run down. I thought I should have been playing but that is neither here nor there.'

Robert Reid is watching anxiously in the crowd.

'When Dalglish scored I began to panic but fortunately the team didn't,' he said. 'On came Johnny Gibson as a sub and he was terrific. He took the game by the scruff of the neck, took the ball for the walk and irritated the Celtic defence.'

'At no time did we feel really safe but then John Gibson came on and that helped enormously,' said Denis McQuade. 'The way Gibby played was very self-assured.

'He was told to come on and hold on to the ball and between him and Alex Forsyth they were playing games and killing time. Gibby loved that because he was very good at it. He did a great job when he came on and we just basically tried to ride the game out.'

The sound, the atmosphere, is changing now too. The Thistle fans are finding their voice. Every pass is being cheered. Cries of 'Thistle! Thistle!' carry through the air.

Rough picks up his hat in the goal in which is wrapped his stopwatch.

'I was quite superstitious I always had a watch with me, a stopwatch in my hat and I knew how long there was to go,' he said. 'I kept looking at the watch as the moments ticked down. With five minutes to go I thought we had won the game. I thought, "Even I cannae be that bad that I'm going to lose three goals in five minutes.'"

To a man the Thistle players begin to think the unthinkable, allowing something they had steadfastly refused to enter into their minds as battle raged – the thought of victory.

McQuade and Rae would fight such thoughts until the final whistle is blown. Forsyth and Bobby Lawrie allow the joy to seep through with five minutes to go.

Even the ever-so pessimistic Hansen allows his mind to turn to thoughts of glory.

'With ten minutes, they can't score three goals then,' he said. 'The crowd started shouting again and believing in us again.

Then you start to think, "We are actually going to win this!"'

CHAPTER 11

THE FINAL WHISTLE

IT IS inevitable now. Nothing can stop the outcome. The Celtic players know it, the Thistle players know it. Every one of the fans inside Hampden knows it. Perhaps even Frank Bough has figured it out.

Celtic continue to throw punches but there is no weight behind them and Thistle can easily bat them away. The only thing that matters now is time and the only watch of any significance is the one around referee Bill Mullan's wrist. He has told some of the players that there are only minutes remaining. Seconds in fact. He puts the whistle to his lips, and blows.

'It's all over, and it's Thistle's cup. A magnificent performance by Thistle who finally, once and for all and emphatically, have put paid to the unpredictable tag. And you can hear the whole of Hampden rising to Thistle,' announces commentator Arthur Montford.

Captain Alex Rae is head over heels.

'I did a wee forward roll, I don't know where that came from,' he said. 'I didn't know what other way to celebrate. I was ecstatic, I knew it was a life-changer without a doubt.'

Arms are raised aloft as the Thistle players embrace. There is a fleeting moment of disbelief. Has this actually happened?

'My first reaction was can we start again because the 90 minutes, it's like you snap your fingers and it's gone,' said Alan Rough. 'I mean, if you knew the score was going to be 4-1 can we start again and enjoy it and appreciate it. Every time we scored it was great but we hadn't won the game so when the final whistle goes you are just walking about wanting to jump on someone.

'I do remember every Celtic player to a man came up to shake our hands. The sportsmanship from the Celtic boys was unbelievable. I remember them going about shaking hands and their manager shaking hands. I think they appreciated what we had done.

'The Celtic fans gave us a great response. It was fantastic. And then after you win it you think, "This is brilliant, we should do this every year! I wonder when we'll be back?"

'We were a wee club and nobody in the land thought we would win. We had no right to win, we hadn't really done anything to justify [it]; we were just young boys still learning.

'To go along there and enjoy the day hoping we would win. When the final whistle went, to this day I could relive it. I wish I would have enjoyed it because you don't enjoy it when there is too much at stake.'

'I went off my head running about daft,' said John Hansen. 'I had never been in that position before and it is hard. You want to run about embracing the rest of your team and at the same time you have to console the opposition because they are still Celtic Football Club, still guys you have looked up to for the last ten years. You want to be courteous to them. I can't remember if I did shake hands with any Celtic players. I just remember the euphoria.'

In the stand, younger brother Alan is cheering himself hoarse. 'I was jumping up and down,' he said. 'I was absolutely delighted. My dad, uncle and I couldn't believe it. Thistle had just beaten Celtic 4-1 in the League Cup Final and my brother had played at right-back.'

'The one thing I can remember is when I came off the park I looked up to the stand and I see Alan,' said John. 'I have never seen the look on his face and at that moment, and I have spoken to him about it because up until that point he didn't want to be a footballer he wanted to be a golfer, I think that day made him realise that this was what he should get into rather than golf.

I'll never forget the look on his face when I came off. He was beaming.'

But the brothers will have to wait until they meet up.

'I never saw him for about four or five days so it was a long time,' said Alan. 'We always took the mickey out of each other so I would have said something like "just as well you're playing with ten good players". He laughed and I think he said, "Tell me again next time you win a major title!"'

'The emotions at the final whistle? First of all relief,' said Denis McQuade. 'In our heart of hearts we were half expecting to be a different team in the second half and that this bubble, our dream, was going to popped at any moment. At the end of the game it was relief then the realisation of what we had achieved. Over the piece we were a far superior team on the day. You need a bit of luck as well but we made our luck that day by being aggressive.

'Our youth and enthusiasm and fitness were the major factors and the spine. Alex Rae was an enormous influence on the game as captain, he kept us going. That thing with Macari – Alex wanted to beat Celtic, he was an immense captain and kept us all on our toes throughout the whole game.'

'It was a bit of disbelief,' said John Gibson. 'We were looking at each other, saying, "Jesus! Did that just happen?" It was euphoria.'

Jock Stein immediately seeks out Davie McParland and offers his opposite number a congratulatory handshake. He is disappointed and already the inquest has started in his mind. He hates defeat but is sporting at the climax. 'Your team deserved it,' he says.

'Everybody believed that Celtic were going to win,' said Jackie Campbell. 'People say Celtic had a bad day but Celtic didn't have a bad day, they just weren't allowed to play the way they normally played.

'They were too busy chasing shadows.'

* * *

ALEX RAE is in dreamland. It is dawning on him as he climbs back to his feet after his roll of celebration that he has one more task to complete in his captain's role. From across the park, amid all the celebrations and congratulations, he can spy a flash of silver amid the crowd in the main stand.

As a kid growing up in Govan he couldn't have imagined a scenario where he would climb the steps at Hampden to lift a trophy.

'When I finished my forward roll that was the thing I was just bursting to do,' he said.

Celtic players have received their runners-up medals and have departed the scene, leaving the stage clear. There are pats on the backs and handshakes and, as he climbs the steps, Rae scans the crowd, picking out faces of family, especially his mother Isa. His father had passed away just a few years before.

'The scenes of joy as you are walking up the stairs lots and lots of older people openly crying, hankies in hand. It was very touching and moving. Such a privilege.'

Alan Rough too can pick out the face of his father some seven or eight rows behind the presentation party.

'Climbing the steps was a blur,' he said. 'You are walking about in a daze, struggling to believe what you and the team have just done. It is just euphoria.'

For Frank Coulston, the march up the steps is a bittersweet moment.

'My father had just died in the January of that year,' he said. 'He was always a keen follower of my career and he would have been very proud that day. It's just a pity he didn't make it.

'I was very happy to be playing there in the first place. Hampden in a final was great and to go up and get a winner's medal was special.'

'Walking up the steps, seeking out family in the crowd, it is a very special feeling,' said Jimmy Bone. 'You expect the big clubs to be going up to get the medals. Every now and then one of the other teams would get it and it just felt like that. I felt it could be a once in a lifetime thing, going up to get the cup. It was a very special moment. We were gibbering, so excited, so pleased.'

'Looking back a lot of it is a blur,' said Ronnie Glavin. 'I can hardly recall going up to collect the medal but I do remember it was the most amazing thing I have ever seen.'

Rae pushes his way through the throng to the presentation party. He is face to face with Lady Tweedsmuir, Under-Secretary of State for Scotland. He couldn't care less.

She offers congratulations and passes him the trophy. As he lifts it skyward his is the loudest cheer in Hampden.

* * *

DAVIE McPARLAND has made his way back to the Thistle dressing room through a tunnel of well-wishers. There will be no lap of honour nor the obligatory team photographs so he knows his victorious players will be joining him soon. Thistle players are not even allowed to keep their cup-winning strips and they are thrown back into the kit hamper to be used again. Their cup-winning bonus is £300 – Celtic get £500 for losing.

Already however this sanctuary is filling up and there is an understandable party atmosphere.

Even journalists have made their way down from the top of the main stand and have found their way in. Nobody minds.

A year ago his team was being beaten by Brechin at Glebe Park in front of 886 fans. Now this. Silverware for the first time in 50 years. History makers. Chairman Jimmy Aitken has labelled the team the Maryhill Musketeers – all for one and one for all!

McParland turns to the *Record*'s Alex Cameron and says, 'In a couple of years we should be quite a good team.'

He then burst into hilarious laughter – and warns his players who are by now trooping in to be careful not to drink too much champagne.

It's too late for Glavin.

'In the dressing room there was champagne flowing,' he said. 'I'm not a drinker. I can recall they filled the cup with champagne, I took a swig and it was the worse taste I've ever had in my life – and I was pissed.

'Whenever you see photos of me, I'm just smiling, everything is going on around me and I'm totally pissed after two swigs of champagne.'

McParland remains in reflective mood. The dressing room is full with players, the rest of the Thistle squad, coaches, even members of the board. There are press photographers too, desperately catching images for tomorrow's editions.

'The players are mostly just laddies,' McParland says to Alex Cameron. 'We lost a bit in the second half because we weren't sure what to do when Celtic hit us as we knew they would.

'This will come. When Johnny Gibson went on in the second half he slowed things down and we took over again.'

Voices are raised as snappers try to pin down the four goalscorers – Rae, Lawrie, McQuade and Bone.

'It was mayhem,' said Bone. 'Everybody was talking, nobody was listening.'

'It was euphoric,' said McQuade. 'We were all looking at each other and laughing. "How the hell did that happen?" We were so proud that we had done such a thing at such an important event. You know now you look back, at the time you think you're going to have lots of opportunities to do things like that and you realise as you get older these things don't happen often.

'It teaches me to tell the players of today to enjoy it, put 100 per cent in your playing time because it is over in a blink of an eye.'

Jackie Campbell is struggling to take it all in.

'It was pandemonium,' he said. 'Celebrating the fact that we won a medal and it is something, that, because it is Partick Thistle it could be a one-off and we'd never do it again.

'You know you are playing in the First Division in a team of part-timers and full-timers. To do that was something out of the ordinary because it was Celtic we were playing. It would be a different day if it had been Falkirk or somebody but it was Celtic.

'We were written off all week because Scottish football didn't get many shocks.'

Alex Rae is celebrating with the unsung heroes of the backroom staff.

'There was Willie Ross, a magnificent wee man, a working man, he'd talk to you like an adult and give you wee gems and diamonds,' Rae said. 'He never let you get too down or too high and absolutely every game at Firhill he would be at the dugout. "Remember Alex, retaliate first," that was his war cry. Jackie Husband had a lot of involvement with the matchday team and his record is unbelievable but as a wise man he was a great influence and inspirational. There was just mayhem.'

The trophy is being passed around the dressing room, over heads and outstretched hands. Still the players are in their strips. They don't want the dream to end. Their laughter and cheers hang in the air and carry out into the corridor where the Celtic team are already making their way out and heading back to Parkhead and home. The loser never wants to hang around for the party but amid all the bedlam, Lou Macari seeks out Bobby Lawrie and shakes his hand.

'We were all friends at the final whistle,' Lawrie said.

The silverware reaches Alex Forsyth and he stares at it in wonder.

'When you are growing up your dream is to play in a cup final and to go and win it, it's part of history,' he said. 'It was the way we won it that was the big thing. Nobody could say we didn't deserve to win – we won that day with good play and good players. They were a good side and we got them on an off day when they were just a bit too confident and we were more up for it than they were.

'Jimmy Johnstone was the best dribbler of a ball in the world. Kenny Dalglish one of the best strikers in the world. Lou Macari, George Connelly a top, top player, Harry Hood scoring goals for fun – they were a team of superstars and I just think they were too confident.

'The congratulations were great. I don't think anybody could have believed how well we played.'

* * *

THE manager's day is not done. There are interviews to complete for radio, television and the press. He exits the party. It is a necessary evil. His voice is showing the strain after an intense 90 minutes but he is happy to dissect the final player by player, almost move by move.

'It isn't really a day for caution, yet I want to stress at the start that this is only the beginning,' he says. 'The victory was the result of hard work, understanding and total co-operation from everyone on the staff. And it has given us our most wonderful day for half a century.

But I know, and the players know, that we still have a long way to go.

'It would be unrealistic to claim we have arrived because there is a cup in the boardroom. It would be naïve maybe to think that we could play even better than we did in that incredible first half.

'We have rough edges. We have faults. And we have a lot of hard work to do yet.

'If I sound over-cautious I'm only being realistic. And I want to get that out of the way before I talk about the victory itself.

'We are improving. We have learned even from the start of the season. But the team is still young. Some could go off the boil. We could have injuries and the primary job is still to consolidate in the league this season.'

But much as McParland is being realistic and desperately trying to keep feet on the ground, there is one thing he can't shake off – the beaming smile across his face. Never could he have imagined when he took the job just 18 months ago that he would be standing here as a cup-winning manager and the team he moulded from the ashes of relegation a cup-winning team.

'We didn't change our style because there was no way we could change it and improve on what we had,' he continues. 'We are committed to an open, attacking type of game because it suits our players best.

'There have been times I've had to contemplate changing this season. We went to Greenock, attacked for 85 minutes and lost 2-0. I had to wonder if we should play differently away from home and decided against it.

'We decided to go for Celtic in the style we play best. I had to allow for the fact that they would probably play three in midfield against my two, Ronnie Glavin and Alex Rae. I reasoned that they would use Jimmy Johnstone there.

'This is where Denis McQuade became a key man and did a wonderful job. He dropped back into the middle when he was needed, yet was still up front to create chances and score a goal. He wasn't the flamboyant individualist the fans expect. He had a job to do and he didn't miss a trick.

'How do you pick individuals from a team that did such a wonderful job? I know we got breaks and losing Johnstone would have affected Celtic badly. But, firstly, we had a great goalkeeper when we needed one. A good save at the right time can lift a team that is beginning to struggle and Alan Rough did that for us apart from being thoroughly competent all the time.

'Jackie Campbell suffered a bad face knock to the point that we thought his jaw had gone. But he never flinched. I would say that moving Jackie to centre half has been the best move I've made with this team. After seven years as a full-back he took time to settle but what a player he was at Hampden.

'Frank Coulston is one of the best players off the ball in Scotland and he and Jimmy Bone got through a mountain of work, chasing the long ones down the wings, spreading the defence and keeping them on the hop.

'But I would hate to miss out a single one of them, even the little ace we had to put on at the right time, John Gibson. He went in when I needed someone to hold the ball and slow it down and what a fantastic job he did. If he seems too good a man to keep on the bench remember the last thing I wanted in the first half was to slow the game down.

'I am delighted to take the League Cup but make no mistake about it, this is just the start. With the win over Celtic we broke a barrier that other Thistle sides had found impossible to get past. We know the feeling of winning a cup at Hampden now – and we will be back for more, believe me!'

Asked if he felt Celtic had underestimated his team, the Thistle boss replies, 'The Celtic players maybe didn't quite understand that we could play a wee bit – and it was too late by the time they made their minds up that we could.'

McParland exits the media huddle and in comes Jock Stein. He does not like defeat at any time but most certainly not in the big occasions. The newspaper boys know this and they tread warily. But Stein is in magnanimous mood and is generous in his praise of the victors.

'I can't take anything from them,' he says. 'They played extremely well and they deserved to win. We have no complaints.

'I know we made mistakes, especially in defence and I know we missed chances. But I still have to praise Thistle. Good luck to them.'

With that he takes his leave, killing time until the stragglers in his team exit the dressing room and make their way back to Parkhead.

He finds himself in the tunnel, solitary and alone with his own thoughts.

Archie Macpherson has by this time made his way back to terra firma, successfully negotiating the journey from commentary platform to pitchside.

'Long after the final whistle, I mean really long after the final whistle, when I came down, there was Stein almost with his hands in his pockets as it were, leaning up against the wall of the tunnel,' he said. 'And I came to him and he looked at me and said, "Well, you got the result you all wanted then, eh?" just like that.

'He wasn't dejected, it was almost as if he had been resigned to that.

He thought we were all biased and add to that that everyone has a kind of affection for the Thistle and I think if you added that to it then, well, you got the result you all wanted. I wrote in a book that any team playing against Celtic in a final was in reality a surrogate Rangers and that is how he thought about it as well.

'After the game Stein went over the hill to the hotel that Bill Tennant ran, I think it was called the Marie Stuart, and he met Tony Queen his great pal and he ended up singing because he fancied himself as a singer so he ended up just accepting it all. I remember Tony saying to me he was like a bear with a sore head to start with and then the mood changed in him, he just got into the spirit and he ended up singing.'

But, much as Stein is sporting in victory and eventually enjoys his evening, in his head the inquest is already starting. Goalkeeper Evan Williams will carry the can.

'Jock didn't like goalies,' said Williams in an interview with *The Scotsman* long after his gloves had been hung up. 'Ronnie [Simpson] and I debated this a hundred times. To him it was like we were a necessary evil. He was never off our backs.'

Denis Connaghan was bought from St Mirren just two days after the final and took over between the posts. Dixie Deans arrived from Motherwell. Stein was shuffling his pack but also the mindset. This Celtic side would go on to win the league, the Scottish Cup and lose out in penalties to Inter Milan in the semi-finals of the European Cup.

In a television interview at the end of the season, Stein confesses, 'I believe, and I try to get my players to believe, lots of people won't believe this, I believe that we are capable of losing the next game we play.

'And I try to gear the players up to the fact that we are capable of losing the next game.

'The biggest blow we ever had as a club was the League Cup final when Partick Thistle beat us 4-1. Not from the defeat – because before the game lots of our players thought that defeat was impossible. That then was the sign to us that things had to change. We needed players who were hungry again. We needed to get going again. We needed to believe that people could beat us. We needed to believe that when we stepped over the white line to start the game we had to make things happen for us.

'In that match we just thought it was a case of going out and things would automatically happen for us. Once that was out of the way it was nearly the end of the season before we lost a match after that.'

* * *

JACK HARKNESS has not left the press box and as he stares out over a now-empty Hampden he is pondering how to begin his copy for the next day's edition of the *Sunday Post*. He had played nearly 300 games for Hearts and been the Scotland goalkeeper in the Wembley Wizards team that won 5-1 against England before turning his hand to sports journalism.

In short, you would imagine that very few things in the game could shock him. Perhaps he would have agreed with you before, but now he is not so sure.

'After 50 years in football I can now say in all honesty I have seen everything,' he writes. 'Yes, Partick Thistle have won a major trophy.

'And today 11 Firhill players – plus substitute Johnny Gibson – can rightly lay claim to having taken part in the club's greatest-ever victory.

'The great pity of it all is that every Thistle fan, who has waited patiently for a display such as this, can't tell his friends anything about it.

'Because long, long before the referee had blown for time-up, every Firhill fan inside Hampden had completely lost his voice! And none of them seemed to care much if they would ever get it back again.

'As goal after goal went in in Hampden's most amazing-ever first half I tried to fathom Thistle's tactics. I couldn't. Simply because in 90 minutes of football they seemed to have 90 different ideas up their sleeves.

'And especially in these first 45 electrifying minutes. Celtic could do nothing about it.

Or at least very little. It was a triumph for youth, for joyous abandon, for team spirit, and for more than a fair share of footballing ability.

Further along the press box, Martin Frizell is dictating his copy down the telephone.

'It took only 37 minutes of believe-it-or-not football at Hampden to establish firmly that the new capital of the soccer world is Maryhill, Glasgow,' he says. 'What a turn-up this was. Celtic's hopes of winning the trophy back after their defeat by Rangers last season were slaughtered by the young lions of Firhill.

'But few of the Thistle fans in the 62,740 – though they knew all along their team would win – could have imagined that Celtic would be taken apart so easily.'

Towards the back of the press box, beyond the wooden tables and row of ringing telephones, in a quiet corner away from the madness, former Rangers and Scotland player Willie Woodburn is in conversation. It would make the basis of his newspaper column the next day.

'This wasn't a dream,' he says. 'It was merely Thistle's bright young trouble-shooters at work with a vengeance.

'Right from the kick-off they sailed into Celtic in rip-roaring fashion and had the Parkhead defence absolutely demoralised by half-time.

'The young Partick side fought for every ball and never allowed their more illustrious opponents to settle down at any time during the game. They moved the ball about smartly when in possession and their running off the ball was excellent.

'It must be a long time since Celtic were beaten by half-time but they have no complaints – they were well and truly shattered before then and couldn't do a thing about it.

'This will go down in the history books as the biggest turn up of the century. But don't forget, there was no fluke about it.'

* * *

Back in the dressing room the Thistle players are now being asked to pose for group shots. The images will go down in club history. Alan Rough has the cup safe in his hands, Jimmy Bone a bottle of champagne above his head. Denis McQuade, in true Thistle style, appears to be drinking his bubbly from a champagne flute while Alex Forsyth is resting a bottle of beer on Jackie Campbell's head. McParland joins the scene, almost on the periphery, in his sharp blue shirt.

It is time to go, time to return to their spiritual Firhill home.

It is hard to get the players to focus. Like herding cats. But eventually they are ready to exit and board their transport back to Maryhill. But the bus that had set off from Esquire House in almost anonymity earlier that day is surrounded by fans cheering and waving scarves.

It would be like this all the way home. The returning heroes.

At the door of the bus, Isa Rae, 5ft 2in of Glasgow womanhood, is in confrontation with one of Strathclyde Police's finest. There will only be one winner.

'The bus journey back to Firhill – the reception from Hampden to Firhill was quite exceptional,' said Alex Rae. 'Celtic supporters actually clapping and wishing you well because I think they understood the quality of football that was played that day. And they had witnessed something that was a wee bit special.

'Almost any time the bus slowed down on the journey to Firhill there was lots of clapping and cheering. It was quite emotional.'I had lost my father about seven years previous. My mother was at the game and after the game before the bus moves, wee Isa, my mother, she was in tears and this big Glasgow polis tried to stop her getting on the bus.

'He was destined to fail. She got on the bus and of course I was close to tears, she was in tears. It really was a very emotional and very special moment.'

The bus is packed. There are twice as many coming back as there was going. The numbers have been swelled by Isa, by wives, by girlfriends. Television cameras have somehow got on board.

The beer is swilling and spilling across the seats and aisles. Nobody is caring. Instead, they are singing.

'We shall not, we shall not be moved
We shall not, we shall not be moved

Not by the Hearts, the Hibs or the Celtic

We shall not be moved.'

'We were off our head, all singing and jumping about,' said Alan Rough. 'Just total celebrations as most teams would do. Just a bedlam of joy. Celebrations were a blur.

'The bus thing was a joke. All cramped on this bus. Twenty going to the game, certainly 40 going back. And then we had the cup. Tradition is the open-top bus but we were in this single-decker and someone was trying to get the skylight on the roof open and it only opened up 50 per cent. People were trying to stick their head out this window.'

But the lack of opportunity to show off the trophy to the fans they pass on the road back to Firhill is not the only thing concerning the 19-year-old goalkeeper.

'A function had been planned win or lose,' he said. 'My main worry was that everybody had partners but me.

'And I had to phone a girl I was at school with to come to the do at night. Linda Gallacher attended and is in the photo at Firhill, she's standing at the end. Maybe I had prompted it the day before. I wasn't going out with her but she was nice-looking.'

Everywhere the players look, out of every window, there are fans, smiling faces cheering back at them. They are hanging off buses, off lampposts, out of tenement windows. Many who had been at Hampden that day are desperately trying to beat the bus back to Firhill. For a lot of them it is a lost cause. A police escort helps the Thistle party speed through the traffic. How different it all is from the journey earlier that day.

'It was fantastic,' said Alex Forsyth. 'For the fans, how could you believe that we would win that day? They must have been over the moon. Even when we came back on the bus to Firhill the whole street was all lined. It was unbelievable.

'We had the cup, singing, delighted. The crowd when we came back, when we left there were a few there and we thought we were coming back to an empty Firhill. We had the trophy and the fans were unbelievable. It was amazing, just amazing.'

There is just one problem. Nobody has the key.

* * *

The players begin to realise something is up when they are told not to get off the bus. The fans by now throng the street, banging on windows and each member of the cup-winning team wants to get out and take it all in. Wait, they are told. Wait.

Behind them, the second bus containing wives and girlfriends arrives. They are equally mystified at what is going on.

'The only thing I remember is that we had to go back to Firhill and the TV cameras were on the bus and we couldn't get in because nobody had the key,' said John Hansen. 'We are sitting on the bus trying to work out what to do. It's just typical Thistle – TV cameras, we've just won the cup and we can't get in.'

Nobody knows what is going on. Certainly not Ronnie Glavin.

'I was still in this kind of dreamland after the champagne,' he said. 'All I could do was try to join in with the songs they were singing. I hadn't a clue what was going on. I couldn't pick the cup up because I was that unstable and that is after two swigs of champagne.'

'I don't know who the key master was but all our stuff was at Firhill,' said Rough. 'We had to change. We all had velvet suits. I had a black velvet suit and a red shirt.'

He also has a date to arrange.

How the matter is resolved depends on whose story you listen to. The popular version is that somehow the key holder was tracked down and despatched from whatever hostelry he was imbibing in. There is another school of thought however that the boot of a giant policeman allowed them to achieve entry.

'There was a bit of scrambling about to get us in there,' said Denis McQuade.

'I remember some of the celebrations. It was a great function and they must have thought even if we get beat we'll still have an enjoyable night. It was incredible. Everybody was on a high. I remember Willie Waddell turned up about halfway through the night, half-cut, to congratulate the manager and everybody on the result. That was quite a pleasant surprise.

'Everybody had an amazing time.

The biggest thing for me was the camaraderie and team spirit that we had as a group and that included the manager. There were no prima donnas. They were a very well-balanced team and that was down to the manager, he knew how to blend youth and experience, speed and guile. Everyone played their part, everybody played to their potential.

'Everybody contributed and it came off. Some days it comes off, some days it doesn't.'

The celebration party is coming to an end. Most, if not all, of the players have headed to parties elsewhere. The lights have come on, illuminating the carnage of what has been a splendid evening. Tables are strewn with the empty glasses, bottles, coffee cups. Davie and Terry McParland are among the last to leave, heading for the door and on towards another gathering of friends. They have not gone far, not yet reached the fresh air of Royal Exchange Square when Terry grabs her husband's arm. 'We've left the cup,' she says. They return to the function suite and there it is, in all its silver glory. 'Aye,' says McParland. 'We'd better take this with us.'

'They had forgotten it and had to go back and get the cup,' said daughter Yvonne. 'They took it up to the pub my mum and dad had on Garscube Road, where the staff and friends had been waiting.'

* * *

It is late in the evening, the party is over and Jimmy Bone is on his way back to Fallin, a combination of train and bus as it had been that morning. He is exhausted. The energy and emotion spent that day is taking its toll. But he is replaying every moment in his head.

'There was a real feeling of joy and satisfaction,' he said. 'It was that wee bit special because it was Thistle, my first club and one of the smaller clubs against the two big clubs in Glasgow and always sort of put down. It was great.

'The Thistle supporters that day – it must have been a sensational day for them to go and watch the game. I remember sitting talking with just a couple of members of my family and just saying, "How does it feel for these supporters, it is a fabulous day for them."

'I am one these guys when you lose you move on and when you win you move on, you don't dwell on it. But I just felt we had achieved something remarkable.

'My thoughts went to the supporters because there were quite a lot who you knew personally. You would see them when you went to away games. You would be chatting to them on a fairly regular basis. My thoughts were for them.'

Alex Forsyth has made his way back to Baillieston after a night of revelry. He is still on a high, all the more so when he realises his parents' house is full of folk.

'We celebrated all night,' he said. 'We had another party in my mum's house. All my friends were sitting there at midnight waiting for me when I got home and it went on all night and into the next day and the next couple of days.'

Intermittently, amid all the celebrations, he too lets his mind slip back to the match.

He said, 'A lot of people underestimated the players we had in the cup final. Rough, Hansen, Bone, Denis – five or six players all would get into the international team. We had some good players. It maybe was not that big a shock that we beat Celtic [as] we would beat Rangers at the start of the season, we could beat Aberdeen. These were all the big teams and we could go and beat them.'

Perhaps the last word should go to the man who made it all possible. Davie McParland had always had faith in his boys. He had prepared them perfectly, made the tough selection calls and ensured that feet were kept firmly on the ground. He had also embraced the fact that people had dismissed his team and used that to his advantage.

'You're written off here, you've nothing to lose just go and play,' he had told them. 'You are capable people, you know what to do, you've done it from the start of the season, getting good results and scoring goals. People are noticing you.

Go and prove it.'

And they did.

After the night of celebrations, and the time with friends in his pub in Garscube Road, McParland and wife Terry returned to the sanctuary of the family home in Milngavie. It is quiet, peaceful, an oasis from the chaos of the day that had gone before. McParland climbs the staircase and opens the door to the bedroom where

Yvonne, Tracy and Hazel have long drifted off to sleep. On their dressing table he places the League Cup trophy so it is there when his beloved daughters open their eyes in the morning, the first thing they will see.

'Tracy and I were so excited because we were that wee bit older but Hazel woke up and her first words were, "What is that thing?"' said Yvonne. 'She was too young to appreciate what it was and that is when we picked up the cup and went through to mum and dad's bedroom.'

Soon Roselea Drive will be filled with journalists and cameras seeking interviews and reaction – follow-ups for the next day's editions. But for now, in this moment of peace and quiet, the McParland family are alone. The girls sit on their parents' bed, each one taking a turn to hold the silver trophy.

'It was a good morning,' said Yvonne.

CHAPTER 12

THE AFTERMATH

ALAN ROUGH is on another bus, heading as always from Knightswood but this time towards Maryhill and Firhill Stadium. It's Monday morning, two days after the final. Heads have cleared and normality is beginning to return. Training for the club's full-time players is at its usual time ahead of a busy week with away games against Dundee and Aberdeen. Manager Davie McParland has decided to take his players away and the remainder of the week will be spent in Blairgowrie.

Rough alights on Maryhill Road and walks the short distance, past the tenement buildings, towards Thistle's spiritual home. He is just about to enter when he recognises two faces approaching the ground. Rough is sure it is Terry Neill and Tommy Docherty.

As he reaches the dressing room some of the other players have already arrived. Rough attempts to inform them of the visitors he has spotted but amid the chatter, which still relates to Saturday's heroics, it is unclear if anyone pays much attention.

For the full-timers it is the normal Monday training session, then back to Firhill and, probably, a walk along to Jaconelli's for a bacon roll. For the part-time players it is back to the day jobs – or, in the case of Denis McQuade, lectures at university.

'I do remember going to a maths lecture and the lecturer announcing to everybody that "Denis had played in the cup final",' McQuade said. 'I got a standing ovation – then it was back to normal.'

'It was a fantastic weekend Saturday into Sunday then back to work on the Monday,' said Jackie Campbell. 'People were just asking, "How did you manage it? How are you feeling?" There were congratulations, only one or two were football supporters and there were no big issues. You'd been and done it, "bring your medal in and let us see it", then it was down to work. I had to go in on the Monday and ask for a half day on the Wednesday because we had to get the bus up to play Dundee on the Wednesday night. Then it was back down the road, then back up to Aberdeen for the Saturday.'

For Jimmy Bone it is back down the Polmasie pit, and Frank Coulston has returned to the gym at Bishopbriggs High School where he is taking an early PE class.

When Rough returns after the morning training session he is immediately called to McParland's office. Had he done something wrong? He enters with a degree of trepidation.

'I've just been approached by Hull City to buy you but the club has decided it's not the right move for you,' the manager says. Rough had been right. Neill and Docherty, the Hull double act, had indeed been here on business.

'You'll get a better club further down the line,' says the Thistle boss.

'I just said thanks very much and walked out, as you do,' said Rough. It would be 14 years of sterling service to Thistle before Rough did get his move – to Hibernian.

Docherty will however get his chance to select Rough. The high regard in which the national boss holds McParland and his team will see him call Rough into the international squad. And Jimmy Bone. John Hansen, Ronnie Glavin, Denis McQuade and Alex Forsyth.

'The cup win triggered off Hull City wanting me and then Tommy Docherty, as Scotland manager, brought me in to the Scotland squad to play Belgium up in Aberdeen,' said Rough. 'The League Cup was a trigger for me wanting to be bought at 19 and brought into the Scotland squad. It introduced me to the national team setup and 12 or 13 years playing international football. That game triggered just being noticed. The game brought attention to who we were and what we were doing. I got the international recognition and was playing with Scotland every month. Ironically that might be one of the reasons I never got a move because the club thought I was so important and they couldn't sell me. If I was to listen to Davie McParland and wee Bertie Auld [who would follow McParland into the manager's hotseat] I could have been sold all over the place. "I could have sold you to Man City, here I could have sold you there." Aye, thanks Bertie.'

That afternoon the Thistle players take the League Cup trophy to Phillipshill Hospital, wherein lies a children's orthopaedic unit. Six-year-old Jimmy Ferns of Ballater Street is in jocular mood and 'boos' the Thistle players as they enter the ward.

'I'm a Celtic fan,' he says.

Captain Alex Rae is in charge of the silverware. 'That was fantastic,' he said. 'We had a hard morning at training and we had to appear on television at night. But I wouldn't have missed that for anything. The only thing I got scared about was the tight grip some of the patients kept on the cup.

'I was in charge of it and we certainly didn't want to leave it behind. Not after 50 years of trying to recapture a major trophy.'

Despite all the distractions the team get a credible 0-0 draw at Dens Park on the Wednesday night. Back at their Blairgowrie base the focus is blurred somewhat. There are games of golf, the odd drink here and there. On the Friday night their preparations for the Aberdeen game are disturbed by a wedding party in their hotel.

'That week was just a joy, playing golf and having a drink,' said Rough. 'I don't know how we drew 0-0 with Dundee. Maybe we focused on the Dundee game after the celebrations of the weekend and said 'let's not have a drink until after the Dundee game'.

'I remember going to a nightclub and a wedding but I'm praying it wasn't the night before [the Aberdeen game] because that doesn't look good.'

'What a racket, we couldn't sleep,' said Alex Forsyth. 'We thought "if we can't sleep, we're going down there to join them all". Half of us were all down at the wedding all night, then up to Aberdeen in the morning, some of us were still half cut.'

Thistle are beaten 7-2.

'I remember wee Joe Harper hit one from about 40 yards into the net,' said Forsyth. 'Then someone took a corner and they scored direct from it. I says to Roughie, "How did you not get that?" He says, "Get what? Och, how many's that?" I says, "I think that's six. I wish that referee would blow the whistle so we can get back to our beds."

'The Aberdeen game was one to forget.'

'It was back to earth with a bump,' said Jimmy Bone. 'We had a target on our back then for what we had achieved.

'Those days playing for Thistle were great. The supporters accepted there were days when things went wrong. They accepted that "that's Thistle" and they actually loved and enjoyed it when you had the good days. During that spell, winning promotion and culminating in the League Cup Final, we were capable of doing that to most of the teams. It was a special team.'

* * *

BONE would be the first of the '71 team to leave. For a club like Thistle, where every penny is a prisoner, an offer in the region of £40,000 from Norwich for the young striker in February 1972 is too good to turn down.

It was a wrench for him to depart.

'I didn't even know where Norwich was,' said Bone. 'I was the first to go. They needed money and I was the only one they had a bid for so I got transferred. The decision was more or less taken from me.'

He would stay overnight in manager Davie McParland's Milngavie home before they would both travel south to finalise the deal. Always the father figure, McParland wanted to ensure everything was right. It's a long way from Fallin to Norfolk, a world away even.

Bone would go on to play for Sheffield United, Celtic, Hearts, Arbroath and St Mirren, among others, even as far afield as Hong Kong and Canada. He would also play for the Scotland team.

Eight years after the cup triumph with Thistle, and thousands of miles from home, he was reminded of that magical day while playing for Toronto Blizzard.

'I was on loan there from St Mirren, I was there about two weeks, and after we played a game this guy approached me,' said Bone. 'In a right Glasgow accent he introduced himself and says to me he was chairman of the Toronto branch of the Partick Thistle Supporters' Association. He said they were having their annual get-together and asked me if I would care to go and be the guest of honour.

I told him that I'd love to do that. So, they arranged the date and I went to the function.

'I couldn't believe it. It was packed. Anything up to 250 people in this hall and everybody sounded as if they had a Glasgow accent. It was like being in Esquire House. It was absolutely sensational. Everybody in the place was a Partick Thistle supporter. They made me feel so special. And so welcome. It was a fabulous evening, one of the best nights ever. They partied that night as if it were the night of the final. Eight years later and this was them partying because I was the first one of the team that they had met. It was great.'

To be reminded of the Hampden heroics is, as always, a pleasurable experience. Rekindling memories of career achievements, of winning against the odds, of friendships made that have lasted a lifetime.

'Look through the team,' Bone said. 'Roughie went on to get all these caps, John Hansen was some player, Alex Forsyth went to Manchester United, Ronnie Glavin went to Celtic, I played at Celtic and the other guys all went on and played for years and years.

'The biggest single thing, I feel, was the blend of the players from the previous manager Scot Symon into Davie McParland. It was the mixture of the older guys and the younger ones and the older guys were really good human beings, good people who were prepared to help the younger ones. Frank Coulston used to talk to me all the time. "Come out of there, son," and if there was a break in the game "see what you did there; try this, try that". And he would talk to me constantly. I know Alex Rae would be talking to Ronnie Glavin all the time. You could hear Hugh Strachan and Jackie Campbell taking to the full-backs so we were fortunate because we had good young players with plenty of energy and we had good old pros who really were top-class. These guys were special. They were the glue that held everything together.

'As a young player it was sensational for me. To this day me and Frank are big buddies. We are still in fairly regular contact.

'We did a job on Celtic that they used to do to us all the time. We reversed the trend because we did a Celtic to Celtic. That sums it up. In the first half we looked as if we would score every time we went up the park.

'That was a belief we found in ourselves and the credit for that must go to Davie McParland. The wee words that he would say throughout the week, that this is going to be a good day for us. He built the belief.'

The Thistle season continues with the usual tale of highs and lows. Celtic visited Firhill just a few weeks after the cup final and dished out a 5-1 thumping.

'I think that was our day for getting it right,' said Davie Hay. 'Maybe Thistle were still celebrating.'

But there was also an 8-3 demolition of Motherwell as Thistle finished comfortably in mid-table. Chances of a cup double were extinguished after defeat to Hibs in the Scottish Cup.

The players knew that Bone's departure would not be the last. Simple economics dictated that Thistle needed to swell the coffers with sales – even if that meant bidding farewell to their greatest assets.

It was also a simple fact of life that elements of the Thistle team simply deserved to go on to bigger and better things. Over the following seasons the group broke up.

Forsyth would become Tommy Docherty's first signing as Manchester United manager, Glavin would move to Celtic, Alex Rae went to Cowdenbeath, Johnny Gibson to Ayr.

'You used to sit there at the end of the season because someone always got sold and you would just sit there, waiting,' said Rough. 'Jimmy then Alex Forsyth, then

Ronnie. I was supposed to go to Celtic with Ronnie but the club decided, "You're not getting the two."'

But there was recognition of another sort. Where before pre-season games had taken the side to such outposts as Brora and Dingwall, Thistle were now box office.

They were invited to the Far East to take part in a series of games involving a Malaysian select side, domestic club Selangor, and Lokomotiv Plovdiv from Bulgaria. The results themselves are academic – 3-3 with Selangor, a 1-0 defeat to Plovdiv and a credible 2-2 with the select side. What is noteworthy is the crowds; 75,000, 45,000 and 25,000 were the remarkable numbers.

'I would struggle to think we all had passports, for a start,' said Rough. 'Just before we left, we brought out the new strip and me and John Hansen had to do a modelling session and I ended up marrying one of them – Michelle McLean.'

Hansen remembers the trip being organised and that they were offered receipts from the gate money or first-class travel and accommodation.

'We thought, "Well there's not going to be big gates in Malaysia so we'll go first-class." To be fair to the guy [the organiser] was phenomenal. Archie Lochrie was walking down the aisle with a bottle of champagne in his hand and McParland said, "Archie, do you normally drink champagne on the plane?" and he said, "I dunno, I've never been on a plane before."

'We had two police bodyguards with us so we're on the bus going to a game two hours before kick-off and the pavements are absolutely full of people walking and heading in the same direction as us. We said to the bodyguards, "Where are they going?" and they said, "They're going to the game." Then we saw the game had been advertised as Indonesia v Scotland.'

'It was holiday mode,' said Rough. 'None of us had been so far from home. We were sunbathing, Scottish boys on holiday. Right away on the beach, no suntan oil, nothing. Everybody was burnt and I mean severe burns. And I'm not talking about when you were young you would have that wee bit red. They just lay in the sun and thought they would be okay. And they were like lobsters. The next day we went and played this game and every time someone went to chest the ball or use their thigh they were just screaming in pain because of the scolding of the burns.'

'I remember Malaysia,' said captain Alex Rae. 'It was unbelievable. In Malaysia it was about 90 percent humidity and I think I lasted about an hour. The place was mobbed. I don't know what the deal was but I'd hazard a guess that as opposed to fees we got all expenses hotels which were taken care of by a middle man.'

On the journey home, Thistle stopped in Athens for a game against Olympiacos. When approached at the airport, this middle man was asked to open his briefcase. 'He must have had about £10,000,' said John Hansen.

Thistle would lose 2-0 to the Greek side in a match that was marred by the physical nature of the hosts and the home crowd of 25,000. But it was an indication of just how far Thistle and their players had come.

An invitation to play in the Juli-Koppen pre-season tournament in Sweden followed where the side were pitched in alongside, among others, Hammarby, Hull City and a legendary Manchester City team.

'It was life transforming,' said Hansen. 'I mean, Man City! Staying in the same place as Franny Lee and Mike Summerbee. It wouldn't have happened if we hadn't won the cup final.'

Denis McQuade recalls that Sweden trip as one of the highlights of his career, mixing it alongside Colin Bell, Dennis Tuart, Rodney Marsh and Asa Hartford. Not bad for a lad who was a student at university and had cost £250 from St Rochs.

Yet there was even better.

* * *

THERE are football stadiums in the world for which the very mention of their name sends a shiver of excitement down the back of any fan, such as the Camp Nou in Barcelona, the San Siro in Milan, the Bernabéu in Madrid. But arguably the one that tops the lot stands in Zona Norte, Rio de Janeiro. The Maracanã is the home of Flamengo but also the spiritual home of the Brazil national team. In the summer of 1972 Scotland had been invited to the Independence Cup – a tournament held to commemorate the 150th anniversary of the Brazilian

Declaration of Independence. To the locals, the madly passionate Brazilian fans, it was known as the Minicopa.

Scotland were drawn in a group that included Yugoslavia, Czechoslovakia and the hosts Brazil. In the opening games they drew 2-2 with the Yugoslavs in Belo Horizonte and 0-0 with the Czechs in Porto Allegre. On 5 July 1972, in a Maracanã Stadium packed with 130,000 fans, Scotland played Brazil. Starting at left-back was Alex Forsyth, on the bench John Hansen, Jimmy Bone, Alan Rough and Denis McQuade.

'After the final that year became a blur, with clubs wanting to play against us because we had beaten Celtic and were the cup winners, and I remembered it being a busy year but what an effect that game had,' said McQuade. 'Tommy Docherty had been at the League Cup Final and was at the semi-final and saw me score goals. Suddenly, along with four or five of the other guys, I was in the under-23 and then went to Brazil with the full squad with Denis Law, George Graham, Billy Bremner and Martin Buchan. It was a dream come true for me. Tommy Docherty told me before the Brazil game, "Denis, you've been very patient, I haven't played you but you're definitely getting on at some point." The game was so tight that he never did but I had no complaints. It was a very exciting time.'

In the end Scotland, against such legends at Tostão, Rivellino and Gérson, held their own until the 80th minute when Jairzinho scored with a diving header.

'Just two years before I was playing in the Combination League,' said Hansen. 'The Combination League to playing and winning a cup final to being on the bench at the Maracanã.'

A fairytale story right enough.

* * *

So, what became of the boys of '71?
ALAN ROUGH remained at the club until 1982, wracking up a phenomenal 631 games before leaving for Hibs in 1982.
JOHN HANSEN would play for the club until 1978 in a career that totalled 324 appearances before injury called time on his career.

ALEX FORSYTH played his last game for Thistle in December 1972 before moving to Old Trafford to hook up with Tommy Docherty having clocked up 109 appearances.

RONNIE GLAVIN left in November 1974 when he joined Celtic after making 226 appearances and scoring 65 goals.

JACKIE CAMPBELL was another one-club man who made 578 appearances for Thistle, playing his last game, a 5-1 defeat to Dundee United at Tannadice, in 1982. He scored a single goal, in a 4-2 win away to St Johnstone in the League Cup in 1975.

HUGH STRACHAN ended his playing career with Thistle in February 1974 in his 175th appearance.

DENIS McQUADE left in August 1978 after 90 goals and 336 appearances when he moved to Hearts.

JIMMY BONE scored 87 goals for Thistle before becoming the first of the cup-winning side to leave when he signed for Norwich in February 1972 after making 156 appearances.

FRANK COULSTON scored 82 goals over 272 appearances for the Jags before leaving for his hometown club of Stranraer in March 1975.Captain

ALEX RAE left to join Cowdenbeath after 150 appearances.

BOBBY LAWRIE scored 24 goals in his Thistle career and made 227 appearances before departing for Ayr United in September 1975.Finally,

JOHN GIBSON left in October 1974 for Ayr United after 16 goals in 162 appearances.

But when they meet up, Firhill is at the forefront of their minds.

'It's as if we've never been apart when we get together,' said Rae. 'It certainly doesn't feel like 50 years. It is quite incredible when you are thinking about your football career, you wonder how long before someone replicates this and 50 years was never in my plan.'

'Fortunately, everybody who played that day, we have had many, many pleasant experiences from what we achieved,' said McQuade. 'It has been amazing how people remember it. The boys are all friends still.

'We were a new team. Two years before that we were relegated. Then the club is playing in 66 games against international opposition all over the place. McParland comes in and forms a new team and two years later we're playing in Europe. That is the message I would convey, that if you get the right balance, put your head down and believe in yourself, you can do great things.'

* * *

IT MAY well have been the most recent gathering of the boys from '71 and it was with sadness that they were together. That morning of 20 July 2018 they assembled to say farewell to a legend.

Davie McParland, the man to whom they owed so much, had passed away at the age of 83 and the crowds that flocked to the church off Saracen Street that morning were testament to the esteem in which he was held.

Sadly, his departure from the Thistle manager's job in 1974 had come about through a breakdown in relations with the club's board. Their previous assurances that Hugh Strachan would be appointed as a full-time coach had been forgotten and, as a point of principle, McParland quit the club for which he had given such sterling service as player and manager.

'Dad never really talked about [the final] to any great extent,' said daughter Yvonne. 'Don't get me wrong, he was very proud of it and very proud of his team and whatever but it didn't affect him that much. It wasn't until the 25th anniversary or the Hall of Fame stuff that he started talking about it again.

'But you'll never ever find a story about how my dad felt about leaving any club he was with. He was very private. And he was just of the opinion "that is that era over", that "I have a wife and family to take care of so it's onwards and upwards". He was very much like that no matter what club he was at. He had no bitterness. His feeling was, "If you have nothing nice to say about somebody don't say anything at all." He was gentleman, he was a good person so he had no malice. It must have been a wrench but he didn't dwell on it. And he did have very strong principles, my dad, so if he thought something was the right thing to do, well, it was the right thing to do.'

The passing of time has not in any way diminished what Davie McParland means to the fans of Partick Thistle FC.

To quote from Tom Hosie and Neil Kennedy's book, *Partick Thistle Legends*, 'Words cannot do justice to the contribution Davie McParland made to Partick Thistle during his 21-year association with the club. The achievements, and success, he sustained at the club may never be repeated again. He was a successful and highly popular player who made just shy of 600 appearances for Thistle, finding the net more than 100 times. As an assistant manager he helped implement a youth policy, which led to a talented crop of young players and, ultimately, the club's greatest achievement.

'Yet when he appeared as a trialist in November 1953, nobody could have predicted that would happen. He put in an impressive performance, scoring once in a 3-1 win against Airdrie reserves, a move that forced David Meiklejohn to sign him immediately after the game. A successful playing career saw him rewarded with a Scotland under-23 cap, although he'd rather not remember the occasion as Scotland lost 6-0 to England.

'When his playing career wound down at the end of the 1960s it was unclear what he would do next, but he elected to complete his SFA coaching certificates to coach under Scot Symon, a manager he would later assist. When Symon departed at the end of the 1969/70 season, McParland took over as manager and, after steering the club back to the First Division, he won the League Cup in the autumn of 1971. Davie deserves the thanks and recognition of every Thistle supporter.'

Ironically, after a spell at Queen's Park, McParland went on to work as assistant to the man he beat in that League Cup final, Jock Stein, at Celtic.

Paying tribute to McParland, Robert Reid said, 'David is a massive figure in the club's history, as a player, coach and manager. His feat of taking a relegated team, turning them around inside a season, then winning a major trophy, which for us happens about once every 50 years, cannot be under-estimated.'

As a footnote to the relationship McParland had with his players, we go to a fish and chip shop in Callander, owned by Johnny Gibson. It is many years after the final itself.

'One Saturday I'm frying away and the girls are serving and the next thing I hear this wifie saying, "Aye, you can tell him that his fish is rotten!"' recalled Gibson. 'And I looked up and I just saw the back of this woman disappearing out the shop. I thought to myself, "I'm not having that." So, I went after her to say, "What's the score here? What is wrong with the fish?" and there was Davie sitting there laughing his head off. It was his wife he had sent in to wind me up.'

Still checking on his boys even after all those years!

'It is hard to say what the cup final did,' said Ronnie Glavin. 'It changed us where we went to a situation where people actually knew you. It gave us the sense of being somebody because you achieved something. The good thing about Thistle was the opportunity we were given by them. Taking us out of the back streets and making us into something.

'The involvement at the club changed you and the success came because we were all willing to work hard with a young manager who was enthusiastic, he was on top of us if anything wasn't right. He just kept everybody on the straight and narrow.'

* * *

THISTLE'S hold on the League Cup lasted until October 1972 when they lost to East Fife.

It's not easy being a Thistle fan.

We're a well-known Glasgow football team,
We don't play in blue,
We don't play in green,
Red and yellow are the colours we love,
The colours of Partick Thistle Football Club,
By the way, we don't fear anyone, anytime, anywhere,
So, Fly the Flags for the Firhill Jags and follow them everywhere.

CHAPTER 13

THE FANS

'At a football club, there's a holy trinity – the players, the manager and the supporters. Directors don't come into it. They are only there to sign the cheques.'
– Bill Shankly

IAIN McCULLOCH

All my family, on both my mum and dad's sides, were Thistle fans (from Possilpark and Lambhill) and we were all in the old stand above the north enclosure that literally shook when there were celebrations. I can still remember that afternoon clearly. I was a young boy at the time and had to go to the toilet at 2-0 to Thistle, so my dad took me. Two Celtic fans were standing next to us in the toilet, and a big roar erupted from the stand. One Celtic fan turned to the other one and said, 'See, told you – one goal back already!'. My dad and I looked at each other a bit glumly until we walked back out the toilet to see my uncle and grandpa rolling down the steps as we had just scored a third. What a day. We all went back to Firhill and they actually brought back the cup that night if I remember rightly – on a bus with some of the players.

One thing that I think is overlooked a bit is how good a Celtic side that was. I would go as far as to say that the Celtic team of that era (plus or minus a few years) was the best domestic side ever in Scottish football, along with maybe the Aberdeen team in the mid-'80s. Another aspect of football teams then was that players stayed at the same club so much longer and really became part of the history of the club. If you look at the 11 starters for Thistle that day, they are all legends of the club.

Of course, one of the stories often told about that day is that at Ibrox at half-time, the cup final half-time score was announced over the tannoy, leading to a stampede of Rangers fans heading to Hampden. I don't really believe this though.

JAMES MACDONALD

I remember the game well, what a day! Went with my older brother and a work-mate. Weeks before it my dentist fitted me with one false tooth and a very small plate. So when Alex Rae scored the first goal up I jumped, my new false teeth flying out my mouth on to the terracing. Sad to say I've never seen it again.

ALLAN M

I was born in 1961 in Hugo Street, Ruchill, just a stone's throw from Firhill. Alas my father, his family and my elder brother were Celtic fans so I never got to enjoy Partick Thistle in the formative years. That changed on 29 January 1969 when, maybe as a treat for my eighth birthday two days earlier, my dad, with his Celtic supporting brothers, took me to Parkhead to watch Celtic v Partick Thistle in a Scottish Cup replay. Final score Celtic 8 Partick Thistle 1 and as the saying goes we were lucky to get one. From that moment on I have been a Thistle supporter, spurning my family's allegiance to Celtic and waiting for the glory years.

My love affair and support continued over the next couple of years via 'lift overs' at Firhill to watch the Maryhill Magyars. In 1971, just two years into my Thistle supporting odyssey, we reached the final of the League Cup, surely this was how it was always going to be?! Alas, at just ten years old I was much too young to go to Hampden, until midday on 23 October 1971 my brother Stephen announced he was going to the game with his pal Johnny Reilly, Johnny's dad and younger brother and there was a ticket and space in the car for me! We piled into Johnny's dad's car, a big Ford Zephyr, and made our way to Hampden. Needless to say, as the token Jags fan among a carload of Celtic fans I was the brunt of the jokes throughout the journey. At Hampden, we took our place in the terraces, in the Celtic end, where else! I was at least adorned with a Thistle rosette and at ten years old was accepted and tolerated among the Celtic support. As the goals rained in the tolerance faded somewhat. At least Thistle played well and most of the anger was directed at the Celtic performance although I didn't completely escape some of the bile. I left Hampden elated fully expecting this is how it was going to be from now on!

JIM SOMMERVILLE

I was at the game with three pals, all wearing Thistle scarves. In those days, crowds weren't segregated, so we found ourselves in the North Enclosure surrounded by Celtic supporters.

No problem, until probably when the second goal went in, and we thought it wiser to pull our collars up a bit higher to hide our scarves! Anyway, full praise to the Celtic fans. Even at 4-0 down at half-time, we had no trouble or animosity from them at all.

I think they were almost pleased for us.

A great day that has been remembered at almost every gathering of Thistle fans ever since.

MONTY BORTHWICK

I was a 15-year-old kid from the Gorbals and walked all the way up Cathcart Road to Hampden Park. My father had a ticket for the stand as he was a Thistle fan originally from Maryhill but my ticket was for behind the goal with all the other Thistle fans. Little did I know I would be watching the greatest performance ever from Partick Thistle, my team.

When the first goal from Alex Rae went in we went crazy on that Hampden terracing. Thousands of Thistle fans going ballistic.

Second goal from Bobby Lawrie and it was mayhem. Some old guy next to me had his false teeth accidentally knocked out in the celebrations and I looked down at the terracing ground to see if I could find them as I saw them flying out his mouth. He never had a care in the world. He tried to say something like 'buck my teeth' but I couldn't understand him for laughing.

It was unbelievable and then it got better when big Denis McQuade got the third. Just then I looked over to the stand and there was my father, both arms up in the air and the biggest smile on his face cheering like mad. This man had followed Thistle since he was a kid in the 1940s and had never seen us win a cup final at Hampden. But there was more to come.

Jimmy Bone stroked the fourth goal in and once again mayhem. By now, you think you're dreaming, but no, this wasn't a dream. Everybody seemed to be saying to the person standing next to them, 'I cannae believe it.' Half-time, and it's party time. Singing, hugging and celebrating.

The second half, we lapped it up. Dalglish got a consolation goal with about 20 minutes left and I heard a fan cry "oh no!" when he scored. I thought he was joking but seriously he thought Celtic might come back from 4-0 down. As if. We nearly made it five straight from the kick-off.

We held out, comfortable winners and stayed to watch Alex Rae lift the Scottish League Cup. That 15-year-old kid can still see it now, all the goals, lifting the cup, the banter of the fans, the sheer joy of the occasion.

I left Hampden on my own and minutes out of the ground this older Celtic fan saw me wearing my Thistle scarf and quickly approached me. Pointing his finger at me he said, 'Young man, never ever forget this day as long as you live.' I think he was giving me a compliment on behalf of my team's heroic performance.

Well, I never forget that day. That 15-year-old kid is now 65.

ALISTAIR COOK

I said to my mate jokingly, 'Three-nil at half-time will do me!' From my angle Alex Rae's shot looked high and I just thought maybe it will hit the bar and give them a fright. Then the net rippled. My dad was at a Clydebank game at Kilbowie. The old half-time scoreboard said 0-4. He just presumed they had got it the wrong way round! Got a pleasant surprise when he got home.

ALAN NIXON

I knew it was going to be a good day when I got my raffle ticket for the time of the first goal on the Whiteinch bus and out came the number 14. It was always my lucky number because it was my house number in Drumchapel. It was about to get luckier. I told anyone who was listening that it would also be the score. Celtic 1 Thistle 4.

Hampden was magnificent and we were all just a bit wary of being slaughtered. The first goes in and we were jumping. The second goes in and we thought we were making a game of it. The third flies in and you had no time to think before the fourth and Jimmy Bone saluting the Thistle fans. Was it really happening?

At half-time the talk was still if we might need a replay.

The second half went on forever and then the whistle. I have never checked a watch as much. I remember the Celtic fans staying to pay their tributes. We were all in a daze and got the bus back to Firhill rather than Whiteinch. Where else would you go?

We arrived just in time for the team to show up. The story about the key to the ground was just pure Thistle. Nothing was arranged. Nothing was expected. We hung around for a bit, grabbed each other and pinched each other. Still got the rosette and the memories of the bright green pitch, the pink surrounds and heroes in yellow holding up a cup.

BOB CASSELLS

I'd started supporting Thistle the year before. Coming from a family of Rangers fans, when I first became interested in football Ibrox was always going to be where I would go, but disillusionment with the Rangers 'traditions' and an introduction to Firhill by a school friend, just as they were getting relegated from the top division, meant that I took the momentous decision to change my team.

August 1970 saw me with my new Lumley's-purchased Thistle scarf in place at Firhill for a season of victories the like of which I've never seen again. It wasn't just that they won games, it was the way they played. They just went out to score goals, they didn't seem to know how to play any other way. And over the course of the season they were putting together the best Thistle team that certainly I've ever seen.

After promotion to the top division and an opening-day 3-2 victory over Rangers at Firhill, qualifying for the League Cup Final didn't come as a great surprise to me – but then I was 16, relatively new to this Thistle-supporting lark and thought that this is what it was always going to be like from now on.

When Alex Rae scored the first goal we were delighted, but we feared that this would spark Celtic into life and we'd end up watching us getting a hammering. When Bobby Lawrie scored the second I think we began to feel for the first time that we could win this thing – as long, please God, as we didn't concede a goal before half-time. The third goal just stunned us. Denis McQuade hacking the ball over the line with the Celtic defence in complete disarray just wasn't something that we could have imagined in our most optimistic fantasies.

We thought, you know what, we're either going to win this or be witness to one of the most remarkable days in Celtic's history and one of the worst in Thistle's. Even as a recently minted Thistle fan, I knew not to rule out the latter. And then Jimmy Bone ran round a static Celtic defender to side-foot the ball into the net. Four-nil. I can't read that scoreline without hearing Arthur Montford's commentary – the complete amazement in his voice was nothing to the feelings my pals and I were experiencing on the terracing when that goal went in. We were 4-0 up in a national cup final against a team that not only completely dominated Scottish football at the time but had been in the European Cup Final the year before. Was this real? Were we dreaming?

At half-time I turned to my pals to ask them was it really 4-0? Had I miscounted? Was it only three we'd scored? We debated it for a while, going over the scorers, Rae, Lawrie, McQuade, Bone, no, right enough, it was 4-0.

We just wanted the second half to end. Preferably as soon as it started, but definitely as quickly as possible. When Dalglish scored we had a few moments of terror as we imagined some kind of Celtic comeback, but suddenly there were only five minutes left to play and we knew we'd won the cup.

Looking back 50 years it's hard to describe how I felt. I was 16, aware that I'd witnessed something amazing, but confident there'd be other days like this in the future. Remarkably, at 66 I still believe this. Which in all honesty has to be the most perfect example of the triumph of hope over experience.

BOB FARMER

I was nine in 1971 and went to all the games at Firhill with my dad.

I was at the semi-final when we beat Falkirk. Travelling to Hampden on the 43 bus, Dad told me it was great that we were in a semi, we'd probably lose but I wasn't to be too upset as I'd have seen the Jags in a semi-final at Hampden and there weren't many Thistle supporters who could say that.

Of course we won, 2-0, and the search for tickets began. One of my BB officers was Bert Niven. His father owned a plumbing business on Garscube Road and he was friends with Mr Aitken, the chairman. We ended up in the front of the main stand (row B, seat 23).

Walking from the bus stop, down past Lesser Hampden, my dad told me we had no chance, Celtic were too strong, we'd done brilliantly just to be in the final and not to get too upset.

We watched, incredulously, as Thistle went one, two, three then four up. I couldn't sit still, madly waving my flag to the annoyance of everyone seated near me. Half-time came and over the obligatory Bovril my dad told me we'd done amazing. Celtic would no doubt hammer us in the second half.

The second half was a blur, the final whistle was amazing, the journey back to Firhill passed in an instant and the wait for the team bus to come back was absolutely joyous. We welcomed our heroes, who seemed as surprised as we were, then walked home to Ruchill.

Best footballing day ever.

RUSSELL CAMERON

I had started at Edinburgh University earlier in the month and the night before the game was at a student party in the city and 'got off' with a vision in hot pants who answered to the name Sally. I told her I was away to the game the next day but we still made a date for that evening back in Edinburgh.

I met up with my Celtic-supporting pal before the match – he was at Glasgow University and had been at the semi against Falkirk with me a few weeks before and was fulsome in his praise of the Jags and their performance that night. What he didn't tell me was that he had slapped a fiver from his student grant on Thistle at 7/1! I would have told him not to be so stupid.

We went off to our respective ends of the ground and I didn't see him for several weeks. I could hardly believe what was unfolding before my eyes and, like most Jags fans, felt at half-time that, inevitably, the ceiling would fall in in the second half. Not so, of course. And the rest is history.

Except that I DID get back to Edinburgh for my date (several hours late) but still managed to meet up and we went out for a while before it petered out, unlike my love for the Jags!

And Jimmy, my Celtic-supporting pal? I could not believe he had put out so much money on a bet against his own team and he said that as the first half goals went in he didn't know whether to laugh or cry. His winnings gave him a king's ransom for the rest of the academic term until Christmas and there were many Indian and Chinese meals that made their way into his flat courtesy of the Maryhill Magyars.

Since then, like the rest of the Thistle support, there has been an awful lot more crying than laughing for me. But we all know you don't support our team because you are a glory hunter.

I discovered after the day that one of my flat mates, an armchair Celtic man, was doing his Saturday afternoon ironing when the second half came on the radio from Hampden. These were not days when full commentaries and build-up to the big game were ten a penny. So, he did not know the score when they started with 'four action replays from the first half'.

My other flatmate was observing!

First replay, Celtic-supporting flat-mate, 'Oh good, they got a goal!'

Second replay, 'God, two goals. Haven't they done well?!'

Third replay, 'Aw Jesus!'

Fourth replay, 'Whit will that bastard [me] be like the night!' as he kicked the lounge door and punched a hole in the wall.

JOHN MORRISON

I went to the game with a group of friends and met up in Reid's of Partick at ten in the morning courtesy of Miller Reid's cousin and fortified by my pal John Dryden's mum's sandwiches. The game went by in a flash of disbelief and, in a daze, we made our way to the Exchequer restaurant where we knew the team were going.

We had our pictures taken with the cup thanks to Alex Rae. We made our way to Byres Road, eventually stumbling home to where my wife was celebrating her 21st party with what seemed like a house full of strangers who I had seemingly invited via Hampden and Byres Road.

My neighbours asked me the next day if I had heard the football hooligans singing at five in the morning. What a night and I have been making it up to my wife for the last 50 years for spoiling her 21st!

BILLY McCALLUM

I travelled to this game with my Jags-supporting dad, would you believe it, in a Celtic supporters' bus from Renfrew! I was a die-hard Jags fan although only eight years old at the time. I was born in Ruchill, but the family moved to Paisley, just on the outskirts of Renfrew two years previous to the famous day. Dad had mates who supported Celtic and travelled on this bus. On the way to the game the bus was bouncing, Celtic fans singing away, patting me on the head, giving me 10p pieces. On the way back after the game you could hear a pin drop. The only people smiling and trying to keep their joy in control were me and my dad, and he had to tell me off for hanging my Jags scarf out of the window while having a huge smile on my face!

ANNE HOPKINS

I wasn't at the game but my father told a story about it. He was a lifelong Celtic fan and a bit disappointed that his two daughters ended up Jags fans. It didn't stop him telling his story.

He had lingered too long in the pub and got to Hampden at half-time to see a friend leaving the game.

Said friend greeted him with 'no point in going in Miney [short for Michael], it's already 4-0'.

'Brilliant!' shouted my dad.

'Not for us, for the bloody Jags!' replied his despondent friend.

Always made me laugh as he told it with great feeling.

TOM WELCH

On a cold, September evening I leapt off the bus and ran all the way home. My dad had refused to come to the League Cup quarter-final against St Johnstone at Firhill that night. And who could blame him? A lifetime of supporting Partick Thistle, he was well used to disappointment. Why should he go to a match where the Jags were already 2-0 down from the first leg?

I threw open the living room door. He was watching *Monty Python* with my mum.

'We won! We won 5-1!' He did not believe me. My father did not believe me. Such was the entrenched view of a hardened Jags fan, he could not possibly believe – even from his only son – that we had reached a semi-final. Only when he switched channels for a late-night local news round-up did he actually believe me.

We sat together in the old North Stand at Hampden not long after and watched us beat Falkirk 2-0 to reach the final. A Falkirk side that was managed by the wily Northern Irishman, Willie Cunningham, and fielded one Alex Ferguson.

When I woke up on the morning of Saturday, 23 October 1971 I knew we were going to lift the cup. The grief of being relegated two seasons before had passed and visits to second-tier grounds in the previous season were now history. That said, we did have fun in my dad's red Escort with my cousin and his son, scarves blowing from the windows as we headed for far-flung places like Forfar or Cowdenbeath.

I stepped out of bed and into the kitchen to find my dad making rolls and sausage. Brown sauce on the table, we both sat down without speaking but exchanged a knowing glance. This was it. I cleared up, he washed up. My mum and my sister were both at work so we moved silently about the house, getting washed and dressed.

Not long after midday, we both sat down in the living room to get ready to watch the football preview programmes, *On the Ball* and *Football Focus*. They began at slightly different times, so with a bit of channel-hopping you could catch the Scottish football segments (about a minute or two long) on both channels. I remember ITV giving a fair assessment of our final, 'David and Goliath' stuff, but the BBC presenter pulled no punches when he mentioned the Scottish League Cup Final. No analysis, no team news. He simply said, 'In Scotland, Celtic play Partick Thistle in the League Cup final, where Partick Thistle of course, have no chance.' Sam Leitch was his name and he was to eat those words.

We climbed into the trusty red Escort about half past one. As we did so, we were taunted by the family right across the road from us. All of them were mad Celtic fans convinced we were in for a drubbing. I could see their point. This was a Celtic team who three years before had become the first British side to lift the European Cup. Who were in the midst of a record-breaking nine league championship wins in a row. Who boasted such talent as Kenny Dalglish, Lou Macari, Jimmy Johnstone and were managed by the legendary Jock Stein.

We anticipated some traffic but there was none to speak of and we drove straight into the main Hampden car park with ease. My dad had a serious heart condition so I expected him to take us to one of the stands. 'Not today, son,' he said as we joined a surge of Jags fans heading for the west terracing. We were in our element, singing and chanting long before kick-off.

In a flash, the teams were out, the game had started amongst deafening noise from our fans. The Jags were fast. So fast, Alex Rae caught them on the hop after ten minutes with an unexpected lob on goal. After 37 minutes we were 4-0 up with goals from Bobby Lawrie, Denis McQuade and Jimmy Bone. As the half-time whistle blew, my dad and I stretched our legs on the steps behind the terracing. It was an eerie atmosphere. I saw one grown man with a Thistle scarf, sitting on the steps sobbing like a toddler. He just couldn't take it in. There was jovial banter with the Celtic fans too, but when one smiled at us and said, 'We can come back from this. We've done it before,' it really did send a chill up my spine.

Celtic came out with all guns blazing in the second half but an amazing display from Alan Rough kept them at bay. Even a Kenny Dalglish goal proved only a consolation. We did it. That young team had achieved the impossible. Partick Thistle 4, Celtic 1.

My dad was normally a very cautious driver but that night we went home at speed. We got back and he picked up the phone immediately. Within an hour our home was filled with family and friends, all of them toasting a great victory. Even Whisky, our bad-tempered Cairn terrier, joined in the fun as he sported a red and yellow rosette. The die-hard Old Firm fans in the company were happy for the Jags. And for my dad. Unsurprisingly, the curtains were closed and the lights were out at our neighbours right across the street.

My dad died less than a year later. I was devastated. However, I was grateful that after he and his team being the butt of jokes for most of his life, he witnessed his beloved Jags put one over on the mighty Celtic, and with style.

HUGH MacDONALD

On Friday, 22 October 1971 I left my work early in Campbeltown and used my thumb to head to Glasgow 135 miles away. I got a lift to the Islay ferry terminal south of Tarbert where I was picked up by a chauffeur-driven limo that had let off one of the Islay lairds, and travelled on to Glasgow in luxury. I just knew that something special was going to happen that weekend. I stayed the night in Glasgow after the final, took a train to Balloch on the Sunday and was picked up there by the Campbeltown Territorial Army Detachment returning from a camp in a minibus loaded with beer.

ROBERT LOCKE

My journey to first Firhill and then Hampden was sparked in 1966 when I was starting secondary school. The feast of football at the World Cup and the playground passion for football, at my rugby-playing school, sparked a desire to see professional football. So when a school friend suggested a visit to see local team Partick Thistle, I was keen to go.

I remember the simplicity of some of the football chants with perhaps an early example of Simon Says, 'Scot Symon says put the ball in the net, put the ball in the net, Simon says.' Also the classic, 'Niven is better than Yashin, Flannigan is better than Eusebio, so bring on the Celts we'll thrash em.'

The disappointment of relegation was replaced with the excitement of watching the new, young and vibrant team of Davie McParland, some of whom were close to my age.

The road to the final was an exciting affair. Lots of goals in the qualifying section and play-off. The expectation of defeat after the first leg with St Johnstone and then their 'gubbing' in the second leg. The Hampden taster against Falkirk. Relegation, promotion and a final in my first few years as a Jag.

So to the final. The R.L. Stevenson quote seemed appropriate, 'To travel hopefully is a better thing than to arrive.' As a fairly new supporter my expectation was hopeful but that history indicated that Celtic would triumph. I boarded the number 43 bus from almost outside my house which had many excited Jags fans in good voice. It's hard to express my feelings about what followed. To be 4-0 up after 40 minutes was unbelievable. I remember at half-time discussing if we could hold out and that Jock Stein would somehow conjure up some magic to snatch victory away. At the final whistle the euphoria of the Jags fans was tangible. An outpouring of emotions from older fans has stayed with me. I thought, 'So this is the life of a Jags fan.'

I was lucky in 2007 to be co-manager of the Knightswood Secondary School U18 (Roughie's old school) Scottish Senior Shield finalists at Hampden. I was able to tell the team of my joy and memories that a win at the Hampden final would bring for them and their families.

Just over 50 years after starting to follow the Jags they still give me a lot of pleasure and, it must be said, some pain.

FOSTER EVANS

Though I lived in Firhill Road with my parents from three to four, I had moved first to Pollok with my grandparents and then Govanhill in 1960. As a result, I had been a Third Lanark supporter until they went bust in 1967. Then me and some pals went to Firhill as a substitute for the Hi-Hi's when I was 12. By 1971 I was an enthusiastic and committed Jags fan.

On the day of the game I got up about 3am to work delivering milk across Kings Park, Croftfoot and Langside in the surrounds of Hampden Park. My colleagues on the milk 'float' were Celtic fans (including my dad) who slagged me throughout about the expected drubbing from their team later that day.

I went to the ground on my own and was amazed how well we were playing – at 2-0 up I was worried we would be murdered for our cheek in establishing such a good lead against a very strong Celtic team.

I calmed down at three then four up. I remember us then being joined by some Rangers fans who had heard the score and were keen to enjoy Celtic's embarrassment.

My recollections of the football are limited to Ronnie Glavin being responsible for the early departure of Jimmy Johnstone and thinking that his and Billy McNeill's absence were probably very important. I know that Jimmy Bone had a torrid time from McNeill at our next league game with Celtic at Firhill.

Though that takes nothing away from a great team performance which also reflected individual skill and flair which now seems like a lifetime ago, which it is.

RONNIE KERR

Saturday, 23 October 1971 – a never-to-be-forgotten day. I was there with a pal and for some reason was confident they were going to do it having seen them dispose of St Johnstone and Falkirk in style.

My wife Marion was not into football but even she was sharing my excitement as I set off for Hampden and she told me later that she had listened to it on the radio and was overjoyed. The game itself was unbelievable as Thistle were brilliant and ripped Celtic to shreds in that first half.

Billy McNeill was out injured but Thistle would have still won. As I said I was in confident mood but even so at half-time my pal and I couldn't believe what we had witnessed. Rumour has it that several Rangers fans made their way from Ibrox to Hampden when they heard the half-time score.

We knew Celtic would have a real go in the second half which they did but Alan Rough and co. held firm and Thistle always looked dangerous on the break. Indeed, straight after Celtic scored they went up the other end and Bobby Lawrie fired in a shot which cleared the bar by inches. It was a long second half but finally the ref blew for time up and it was euphoria for the Thistle fans. There was no segregation then and some of the Celtic fans around us took it very well, in fact one or two were shaking hands with us and saying how well Thistle had played.

We went round to see the players getting on the bus with the cup and then I went straight home. Marion had made a banner with the score on it and she was as excited as I was. She even watched the highlights with me later. I was on cloud nine for weeks afterwards and it really was a never to be forgotten day.

RONNIE PEDDIE

On the morning of 23 October 1971 I was walking home with my pal, Ross Lochans, following a wee boys' game of cub football at Scotstoun. He told me that his dad was taking him and his brother to the cup final at Hampden. I was stunned and told him that I was 'dead jealous' as my dad had been a Thistle season ticket holder, but he had died in 1969, and he would have taken me to my first Thistle game.

Within half an hour Ross appeared at the front door holding a fistful of complimentary tickets. 'My dad wants you to come to the game and keep me company.' My mum took some persuading but at 1pm I was going to my first professional football match!

I was delighted to find that our seats (Bank of Scotland complimentary tickets) were right in the middle of the old main stand about four rows behind the Royal Box. I was worried about 'wee Jinky' Johnstone but early on he was clattered by Ronnie Glavin.

What was I concerned about; we were already two goals up and soon we were four goals up. This was absolutely magic!

At half-time Mr Lochans was worried that we might get battered in the second half and lose 5-4. Chance after chance was thwarted by Alan Rough. At the end I was standing up on the polished mahogany seat with my brand new woollen scarf in the air (50 years on and I still use it!). When Alex Rae lifted the cup I was close enough to touch the players!

After the game we took the bus to Maryhill and joined a massive crowd waiting for the cup and the team bus to arrive. The atmosphere was euphoric. When the bus arrived the League Cup was sticking out of the front skylight. Very soon there was confusion as no one had the keys for Firhill and we were told to go home. But we didn't go home, we went to Knightswood to see Mr Lochan's father and dance around his living room. Eventually, I arrived home at ten o'clock and told my mum, 'That was the best day of my life!' We then sat and watched the highlights on *Sportscene.* I looked forward to a lifetime of success and the many more trophies to come. If only!

MICHAEL MARTIN

For those of us who wept in awe on 23 October 1971 those moments are forever. Fifty years on I can relive the emotions of that day.

We set off in celebration of reaching the final, fanciful hope chasing impossible dream, but in cold expectation of the bite of reality. Our opponents looked forward to a stroll and the pundits so memorably wrote us off. The just promoted team facing the lions of Lisbon. Boys versus men. The whistle blows. We are off.

Rae scores – a murmur of appreciation; no more than an irritating setback for our friends from the east. Lawrie scores – looks of bemusement exchanged. At 4-0, might it be the realm of impossible dreams? But despite what might now be said believe me none of us thought it was done. We awaited the onslaught that would surely follow after Mr Stein had had a wee word at half-time.

But still we continued to see them off. And then King Kenny, possibly the most accomplished player our country has ever produced, scores. I looked to the heavens to see if the sky was about to fall in. But the deluge never came, the minutes passed, and we did indeed begin to dream the impossible dream.

In primeval time before internet a tannoy crackled into life at that other place in the south-west of the city. A cough and splutter followed by, 'Here is the half-time score from Hampden. Celtic 0 [a mutter of approval from the hordes] Partick Thistle 4.' Silence. 'I'll just repeat that.' Bedlam. It is said some immediately set off to Mount Florida in salivating expectation. I cannot vouch for this myself but it was told to me by an old friend who was there, now a Knight of the Realm, so it must be true.

It happened with less than ten minutes to go. It started with a rumble in the upper terrace of the North Stand – the stomping of feet. The noise grew as an acoustic Mexican wave swept from the stands to the terraces. The rumble became a roar. Our band of brothers on the pitch momentarily paused and looked towards the crowd in puzzlement. Then they knew, as did we, that the sky was not going to fall in, that this was their day, our day.

The final whistle blew. An explosion of joy was fused with a numbing sense of realisation. It had been done. It had been done. I was there with my family, Jags for decades. My bewildered English girlfriend retold how we all went puce. She feared for our wellbeing. My dear wife saw only one Thistle game in her whole life.

I do not remember the journey back to Byres Road except for absolute celebration and the warm congratulations of all, who knew they had seen something extraordinary, never likely to be repeated. Did we walk or bus it, I do not recall, such was the euphoria.

We retired to the Aragon, welcomed in applause on our arrival. It was simply dreamland on those old leather couches of university days. Now we had in our party that day another bard of Dumfries, but more McGonagall than Burns in style. He had been silent for a few minutes, but then raised a quill finger.'

Hark the herald Partick Thistle,

Glory to our football team,

Goals don't come from one alone,

Rae, Lawrie, McQuade and Jimmy Bone.

Cue boundless hilarity with rendition after louder rendition. We were of course with great solicitude politely invited to move on. As we travelled along Dumbarton Road and Argyle Street into town in glorious revelry I was struck by the overwhelming good nature and bonhomie of those we passed. There was no rancour, no tribal footballing abuse, just a recognition that this was a special Glasgow moment, wholly unexpected in outcome and in style.

We found ourselves in George Square where those august and granite sentinels have stood guard in presbyterian silence, it seems forever. Nothing had moved them in my lifetime. Yet one had wrapped a Thistle scarf around his neck and I like to think I saw a tear running down a stony cheek.

DOUG McNEIL

I was just 14 when we won the League Cup but had been following the Jags for a few seasons. The real love affair started when we got relegated the season before.

This coincided with my dad getting a car which allowed us to travel to far flung places such as Kirkcaldy, Methil, Arbroath, Stenhousemuir and Alloa.

We had a great team and were free-scoring which made the journeys all the more enjoyable. I had every confidence we would do well in the Second Division as everyone assumed we would have a fragile team, but none of that. We surprised most by attacking from the outset and with a great shape we seemed to have an answer for every game with Frank Coulston and Jimmy Bone forging a great partnership up front and being supplied with great wing play from Bobby Lawrie or Denis McQuade or great work from Ronnie Glavin or Alex Rae in midfield.

Alex Forsyth and John Hansen attacked and did great defensive work and with a rock-solid partnership of Jackie Campbell and Hugh Strachan the defence was formidable. And if teams did break through, we had Alan Rough producing miraculous saves. Promotion seemed inevitable, and it was. So rolling into a successful League Cup campaign was just logical.

In the early stages we played some of the teams we had beaten in the Second Division and then progressed on to St Johnstone, Falkirk and then Celtic in the final.

This was big. Sure, we had a good team, but we were in with the big boys now. Although I have never been a Celtic fan I had been pleased with their progress in Europe and their team was very strong. But being very naive I just imagined the thrill of playing them and could only think of the 'what if' scenario. It's just 11 versus 11, right?

Dad got us tickets somehow. He went for Main Stand tickets rather than being in the terracing as he may have been concerned for my safety. A few days before my older brother-in-law said he would like to go. It seemed a bit late but somehow my dad managed to squeeze one more ticket from the club by telling them John was a bachelor of divinity and not very bright – and he had forgotten to get a ticket early. It worked!

He was not next to us but about ten rows in front. We were at the western end of the stand, almost on the goal line but about halfway up the stand, so watched us score four in the first half with ease. Finding John when we scored was not difficult as when we stood up to celebrate, we realised we were in a sea of grim-faced Celtic fans.

The journey home, with the cardboard cut-out of the cup covered in silver paper and two large red and yellow paper flowers stuck in the front window, was fabulous. I don't think I stopped smiling for weeks!

JOE KEARNEY

I was only 13 and already around five years into this love affair when it all happened. My brilliant uncle, John Findlay, had already worked his match-making magic years before, ably assisted by 'lift overs', pies, macaroon bars and spearmint chewing gum. That glorious day, we travelled together along with my cousin Charlie (a Celtic fan) on packed blue train from Glasgow Central to Mount Florida and were well outnumbered by Celtic fans – who in the main, wished us well but offered us 'nae chance'.

Earlier that day, my beloved gran had waved us off as we boarded the 'corpy' bus from Balmore Road. She had been somewhat supportive throughout the cup campaign. 'Flash in the pan, just a flash in the pan,' were her words of wisdom after each win. I think she only wanted to manage my expectations although at the time I thought otherwise.

When the final whistle blew that day, I just sat in my seat in the main stand completely and utterly exhausted, content and never having to ask God for anything ever again. As Alex Rae climbed the steps to lift the trophy, my uncle John reminded me that I should watch Alex lift the cup as I 'might no' see it again'. I quickly stood on my chair and watched him raise the gleaming trophy with its beautiful red and yellow ribbons. The tears ran down my face in a way only a 13-year-old can.

They are still running 50 years later when I think of that day. Then I smile, remembering that when I got home, I ran to see my gran and shouted, 'It's no' a flash in the pan noo is it!'

GERRY BROWN

I was aged 13 and went to the match with my dad on the Milton Supporters' Club bus of which I was a member.

I came from a school with hundreds of Celtic fans and never forget the pounding I took all week about how many goals they would score and we had no chance against the mighty Celtic (I was the only Jags fan in the whole school).

Funny enough I was really confident we would do it. Anyway, we got to the match and we were seated in the front row of the old South Stand among the usual thousands of the opposition fans (no segregation in those days). Great view high up and then the first goal went in from Alex Rae. Great, at least we've scored. We're playing well then the second goal goes in from Bobby Lawrie. Magic! Jeez, another goal from Denis McQuade and only 20-odd minutes gone!

I thought, 'If we could only get another one we might win this!' We were standing up after each goal and applauding as if Thistle did this in every match but then the bottles started to be thrown down from the back of the stand at us at the front. They didn't hit my dad or myself but went close. It wasn't pleasant but we didn't care at this point and then unbelievable Jimmy Bone rolled in number four. We were in heaven; 4-0. And then as every Jags fan will tell you at this game, we could still lose 5-4!

The second half we were watching time and counting down every minute. Celtic scored late on but we knew we had done it. What a feeling when the final whistle went and by that time, to be fair, the Celtic fans that were left were coming up and congratulating us although they were in shock!

Back on the bus among the faithful we were all over the moon and singing, standing up and shouting all the way back to Milton with banners and scarves hanging out all the windows and my memory of the journey back was people on the streets applauding the bus all the way back through Glasgow.

I'm 63 now and my dad is long gone and I still support the Jags but that day will never be forgotten and I'll look forward to the 50th celebrations and think of the great day out with my dad.

BARRY ADAMS-STRUMP

I was born and brought up in Lambhill and have been since the age of three a Jags fanatic. For me football begins and ends with Thistle (maybe a little bit of Scotland thrown in). Having seen many of the group games, I attended the quarter-final against St Johnstone and watched with family and with great glee our 5-1 trouncing of St Johnstone then with equal delight Denis McQuade scoring twice in the semi-final against Falkirk. Saturday, 23 October came and I took my then-girlfriend to Hampden decked from head to toe in red and yellow. 'You are not going out with that,' was her father's reaction to seeing me but off she went for her first ever match. The goals went in – one, two, three, four; I couldn't believe it and like many other was not confident at half-time. Celtic could score four in the second half but thankfully they did not.

I was drunk without taking any alcohol. I remain a Thistle fanatic, was the crowd doctor at Firhill for 11 years and am a member of the 1971 club. My then-girlfriend has been my wife for more than 45 years and has seen us lift several lower-league trophies since but nothing has been as great as on 23 October 1971. My sons say I was very fair – I gave them a choice as they were growing up, they could come to Firhill and watch Thistle or they could stay at home and not see any football. They chose the former.

ALAN HENRY

On 23 October 1971 I had been married for six weeks and so a few trade-offs had to be negotiated to allow me to go to the final.

My family had moved to Prestwick from Maryhill in the 1950s and I remember my dad taking me to the Thistle against Hearts League Cup Final in 1958 – a 5-1 defeat took quite a while to get over but by this time I was indoctrinated into the Thistle way, where you learn early on in life that disappointments happen.

A friend of mine agreed to go with me to the 1971 final and we left Prestwick in plenty of time to get to Glasgow, park the car and go for a pre-match pint. However we hadn't got far beyond Monkton when his Morris Mini decided to cough, splutter and grind to a halt. Well that was it – no game for us. My friend was pretty resourceful and after a few kicks and shoves and full choke the engine spluttered and started. I told him not to take his foot off the accelerator until we got to Hampden.

This was the heyday of football – when you could turn up at big matches without a ticket. We decided to go into the standing enclosure below the main stand at Hampden. It cost a bit more, but who cared, this was Thistle's big day.

Now, it turned out that there was a noisy contingent of Jags fans directly above us in the main stand, well oiled and having a great time before the inevitable defeat. Thistle scored their first goal on ten minutes and above us they went wild. I looked up and a well-stocked bar had suddenly materialised (how times have changed). Thistle scored their second and half bottles and cans were appearing as if by magic. When we scored the third, drink was getting passed down to us and who was I to refuse? The fourth went in and all sense went out the window. It was never-to-be-repeated joy; no bad language, no anti-social behaviour, just unbridled happiness.

DAVID WELSH

In the summer of 1948 I asked my father if we could go to a football match. He said, 'Well we'd better go to watch a local team,' and so my life with Thistle had started. Twenty-three years later I bought tickets for my fourth Thistle League Cup Final and made my way over to Hampden with Aileen, my wife of a year or so who had just found out that she was expecting our first child. On the way along Allison Street I remembered I hadn't put on a bet. I dashed into the nearest bookie and when back in the street Aileen asked if I had put something on 'for the baby'. I remember saying, 'Listen dear, I don't mind throwing away one pound but I'm not going to throw away two.' We were seated at the Thistle end of the main stand so had a glorious view of the first-half goals – one, two, three, four! A nervous half-time was spent wondering how many goals Celtic would get in the second half. But it was only one and the cup was ours! Unbelievable! Hampden was a sea of red and yellow, as was everywhere we went for the rest of the day. Firstly, a lift by Malcolm MacSween, my Firhill season ticket mate, back to the Arlington Bar in Woodlands Road, our usual post-match drinking den. Another sea of red and yellow. A couple of pints later (honest, Your Honour) and then off by taxi to the Stakis Steak House at the Pond Hotel. Guess what, another sea of red and yellow and a well-deserved and greatly needed meal. On the way out of the restaurant Aileen said that there was smoke coming out of my jacket. And so there was! In my excitement I had put my pipe in my top pocket, not checking to see if it was out. No great damage – just a hole in my jacket.

I was determined to call in at Cammie Stewart's house before anything else. He, Alan Robertson (the Doc) and I used to go to Firhill every match day and he hadn't been able to get to the match. In addition, his father, old Jimmie Stewart, had taken us up there for a few years so to thank him I bought a half bottle at the Pond Hotel off-licence and took it up to him to enjoy during the TV programme later that night.

Back in a taxi to the Arlington, dropping in at the café along the road to leave ten bob for Davy Main, one of the only pupils at Woodside who supported Thistle. Another couple of pints and then up to Dave Brennan's in Napiershall Street to watch *Sportscene* or whatever it was called in those days. And then a taxi back home after an unbelievable day!

One day the following week I dropped in to the bookies in Allison Street to collect my winnings – £8. Just about enough to cover the post-match celebrations.

If only I'd listened to my wife!

ALEXANDER THOMSON

The seats in the South Stand must have cost a fair bit. But I think my mate Alan and I both knew that this might be a once-in-a-lifetime opportunity. After all, it had been 50 years since the Jags last tasted cup success. Both of us were married with young families, but we had fixed up babysitters so that our wives could join us in the posh seats.

That first half was like a dream. Alex Rae's looping shot from just outside the box, then Bobby Lawrie's scorcher and big Denis's stab in through a crowd of defenders. After all that the Celtic defence was in tatters, and Gemmell, Hay and co. were rooted to the ground when Jimmy Bone strolled through the gap to score the fourth.

Years later I met Alex Rae when he was working in Fife and he told me that, in the dressing room at half-time, Davie McParland said, 'If we can score four goals in the first half, they can score five in the second half.' Fortunately, they came nowhere near it, and never looked remotely like it.

I was doing a college course at the time, and really enjoyed turning up on the Monday with my Jags scarf on and winding up the Celtic fans.

JOHN WRIGHT

My story starts in 1953/54 when I was 13 years of age and about to be taken by my dad for my first visit to Hampden Park to see our team, the Jags, take on East Fife in the League Cup Final; we lost 3-2 and trudged home dejected.

Then back again to Hampden in 1956/57 when we nearly beat Celtic in the first game which ended 0-0, only to lose the replay 3-2. So, once more, off home disappointed.

In 1958/59 we held great hopes for third time lucky for a League Cup win but it was not to be. Hearts beat us 5-1 and we all felt it was the end of the world that day. I was beginning to feel I would never see my beloved Jags lifting a trophy above their heads at Hampden.

Then our day of glory arrived in 1971, when the sun shone and we all danced our way home with a League Cup trophy. I was on my own that day; my dad had died and could not share this great moment with me. I was in the centre stand to witness it all and then a lovely touch after the final whistle. I had been sitting next to four priests for the match and each one shook my hand and told me what a great team we had. That made my day.

DAVID WATT (BALL BOY)

I could have been a Jags fan.

The second football game my father took me to was Partick Thistle overcoming the Czech side Spartak Brno on a cold winter's night in November 1963. It was a great European night, an exciting game, goals and thrills throughout. Even so, it wasn't able to compete in my mind with the first game I went to – Celtic v Real Madrid, a friendly played a year earlier. I was to be a Celtic fan.

However, in October 1971 I was not only there for Thistle's semi-final and final in that season's Scottish League Cup. I played my part. In the games against Falkirk on 6 October and against Celtic on Saturday, 23 October I was a ball boy. Indeed, sometimes I think I was THE ball boy.

Back then returning the ball to the field of play at Hampden Park was one of the most sought-after 'ball-boying' jobs not just in Scotland but across UK football stadiums. Over 70 applicants for 15 places (12 for a game and three reserves). It wasn't just the sheer joy at participating in the games with the amateurs of Queen's Park whose home was at Hampden. In addition Scotland's national stadium hosted international fixtures, prestigious friendlies and cup tournaments. Real bonus games for the successful ball boy applicants.

The first perk of the job was being able to stroll through the crowds at the front door at Hampden on matchdays. Before games fans would be there waiting around for team buses or checking out guest arrivals. A few quick steps into the entrance, a nod to the blazered club secretary then across the hall, through the glass panelled doors and then past the inner sanctum of the dressing rooms; home team to the right, away team to the left.

Before games ball boys at Hampden assembled in their room at the bottom of the stairs below the dressing rooms and across from the officials' room. Players would walk past our door to get down on to the field for a look around at their state-of-the-conditions. This was the best opportunity for the team of ball boys to pester the stars of the game for their autograph. In the semi-final against Falkirk my autograph tally was high. Several Thistle players kindly added their signature on my programme and the centre-forward for Falkirk, one Alex Ferguson, obliged too.

That night I adopted the belt-and-braces approach and left my autograph book on the small table just inside the door of the Thistle dressing room to collate some more names in the little blue book. Of the Falkirk game I remember little though for each semi I was operating on the touchlines at the sides of the pitch.

Having been on the sidelines for the semi-finals I had the choice between the Mount Florida end or the goals in front of the east terracing. Celtic fans would have the east terracing to themselves, while the west end (naturally) would host the Thistle fans and Celtic support too. Given the shared arrangement then it was the west for me. My reasoning being that the Mount Florida end, with opposing fans aside each other, would offer a better cup final atmosphere.

Once the game started there was little atmosphere as a result of the Thistle onslaught; an attack of shock and awe. Each attempt from a Thistle player, no matter the distance from goal or number of defenders around them, resulted with the ball in the back of the net. By halfway through the first half both sets of fans were oddly silent. The Jags were winning, already two up.

Not many people realise that as a ball boy there are few occasions you are required to kick the ball in guiding it back to the game. The job mostly requires handling skills, throwing the ball back or rolling it towards one of the players. However, this game required a kicker's intervention to ensure Thistle's mauling of Celtic could continue.

My vital contribution, well my vital double contribution, came with goals three and four. Each one crossed the line then trundled and nestled in the back of the net. In each case the ball slowed to a dead stop. It seemed to me that time stood still. It was quiet. You can still view a teenage ball boy toe-poking a ball with greater effect and exasperation in game highlights.

By the fourth goal the Thistle fans were wild in disbelief and joy. Celtic fans were still there; silent observers of their annihilation.

At the end of the game, ball boys changed in their room below Thistle's dressing room. Shouts and songs of joy were continual for 20 minutes or so after the game. We changed and waited outside the door to complete our autograph requests.

When Thistle left I entered their dressing room surveying the littered mess of their celebrations. Two empty champagne bottles were scattered on the floor. It seemed obvious to me these were irreplaceable souvenirs of an earth-shattering victory. In those days you could still get money back on ginger bottles; it may have crossed my mind that champagne bottles might also have a cover charge.

Back home the programmes, the autograph book and champagne bottles were all duly admired by Thistle-supporting team-mates of the club I played for at the time. I gave one of the champagne bottles to a Thistle fan and never ever tried to get any money back on the other. It was disposed of sometime later.

I still have the programmes from the semi-final and final. That old autograph book has a couple of pages with the scrawling signatures of the Thistle team. On occasion to this day when in conversation with Thistle fans I let them know of my crucial role in their team's victory on that October day at Hampden.

GAVIN STEWART

Less than a year earlier, aged ten, I had been allowed to go to an away match on my own for the first time. Coatbridge by train – I got lost between the station and the ground, missed the first 20 minutes and we lost 1-0 to Albion Rovers. An early taste of Thistle hell. It was also my first year of having a season ticket and being an ever-present at home games.

Now we were in a final. I had been at the glorious home leg of the quarter-final and the rather ghostly semi-final at Hampden. So, I classed myself as a seasoned supporter. But because this was Celtic my mum wouldn't let me go because of the risk of trouble. After some serious tantrums, she gave in and got her friend Harry to get two tickets – the deal was she would come with me or the first time! What she hadn't thought through was Harry's persuasion – the tickets were for the South Stand and I was the only speck of red and yellow in an ocean of green and white. Though I was too excited just being there to notice them much.

When Alex Rae popped in the first goal my celebrations were allowed. The man behind us said, 'Don't worry Missus, let him have his fun while he can.' At the second goal he muttered something similar through clenched teeth. By the time Jimmy Bone walked the ball into the net for the fourth my mum knew what she had to do. Her hand was over my mouth to stifle my shouting and she was leaning on top of me stop me jumping up. I didn't care. It was pure unadulterated joy. Absolute Thistle heaven.

At half-time I sat and thought to myself we had probably scored enough to get a draw. I didn't believe Thistle were allowed to beat Celtic. But in the second half I remember we had numerous chances to score even more. When Dalglish finally scored for them it seemed like the whole world stood up. 'There's a lot of them,' I realised. I reckon they still thought they could at least get a draw, though by then I was getting cautiously optimistic.

By the time the cup was presented we were sitting pretty much alone. There had been a very gruff 'congratulations son' from a couple of the departing hordes. But mostly just stunned silence.

As we went back to our car a passer-by asked the score. 'Four-one,' I piped up. 'To Thistle.' 'Aye right, son,' he said. Even when my mum confirmed it, he just laughed and walked away.

She didn't come to another match until the 2002 semi against Rangers. Unfortunately, her status as a lucky mascot hadn't survived the years.

TOM MACADAM

On 13 September 1971 Dorothy and I got married. Seems like yesterday and we know what a crap day yesterday was. Anyway – there then followed two weeks off work for our honeymoon. However, all was not lost as we were back in time for the game. I took my new wife with me for her first experience of watching Thistle. And what an exciting time we had! With about ten minutes left of the game my wee brother nudged me and said, 'Do you think we can hold out?' I replied, 'I don't know.' Well we did hold on and had a wee celebration that night. What a great team we had then. Packed full of internationalists and superstars. Will this be Thistle's year? Well 1921, 1971, 2021. It could be.

MURRAY MACADAM

Back in 1971 I was a 21-year-old student and a couple of years earlier I had decided to get a bit fitter so I joined Lenzie Rugby Club despite not really enjoying being a forward at school, so I called myself a back.

Over the next two seasons or so I began to enjoy my new rugby career and slowly made progress from fourth XV up the ranks to second XV and apparently playing quite well. On Tuesday, 19 October 1971 I was informed by the club captain after the training that I had been picked by the selection committee to make my debut at inside centre on the following Saturday, 23 October, for the first XV. I had to appear before the committee on the Thursday night to explain that I just couldn't play as my wee team were in the cup final that day and while we would be well beaten I just would never be able to get over it if they won. The committee were not happy and were in agreement in only one thing, my team would be roundly beaten. Me, my dad and brother Tom all went to Hampden that day; what a great call.

I did make my debut a few weeks later but never for a minute regretted that decision. I can't imagine how I would have felt if I had made the other choice.

JAMES SHAW

The game for me started at work on the previous day, when a Celtic supporter asked me who I thought would win. And naturally I said the Jags. He replied, 'I'll give you 10/1 they don't!' What could I do, so I took the bet.

Saturday dawned, my brother-in-law and I headed for Hampden with a light refreshment in our pocket. Our seats were in the main stand – row AA, seat 80. Price £1. That was at the end where all the goals were scored.

As the game progressed and the Jags went a goal up, a Celtic supporter behind us sarcastically remarked that Celtic would win by at least two goals to one. The Jags scored again and his comment was Celtic would win 3-2, then 4-3. When the Jags scored their fourth goal I waited for his usual retort but when we turned around he had disappeared. I think maybe he had enough, thank goodness.

In the second half we contained Celtic but threatened them on the break with wee Johnny Gibson coming on to hold the ball up and keep their defence occupied. Then came what all Thistle fans had been waiting for – the glorious sound of the final whistle. 'Ecstasy!'

Monday morning at work, a Clyde supporter told me that at Shawfield when the half-time results went up on the scoreboard it showed the Jags winning 4-0. But everybody thought it was a mistake and it was Celtic leading by that score. It was announced over the tannoy that the scoreboard result was correct.

I still have the old *Sunday Express* report of the match and my ticket for that wonderful game.

And yes, I collected on my bet!

GEORGE CHEYNE:

My name is George, and I'm not a Partick Thistle fan. There, I've said it, I'm coming clean after living with my guilt for 50 years.

It's more of a guilty pleasure, actually, because going to Hampden with my dad to see Thistle win the League Cup in 1971 was one of the best days of my life.

It started off as a homage to my grandad – a lifelong Jags fan who had passed away a couple of years before – and ended up being an amazing shared bonding experience for my dad and I.

The build-up to the game was pretty low-key. That was mirrored in our house as my dad tried to keep a lid on any expectations.

'We're up against a team that got to the European Cup Final last year,' he said. 'I just hope we don't get embarrassed.'

To be fair, he wasn't alone in thinking that. I don't remember many people giving Thistle an earthly ahead of the game.

I had just turned 13 a few weeks before, so it was a huge deal for me. My first final – I couldn't wait.

The excitement of the big day got to me and I woke just after 6am, went downstairs and found my dad in the kitchen. He couldn't sleep either.

He made me a huge bacon and melted cheese sandwich – it was too early for the roll delivery – and a mug of tea. The breakfast of champions, as it turned out.

We chatted away about my boys' club football, school, my younger brothers, the weather; anything, really, apart from the game.

That was about to change, but not because we saw the BBC *Grandstand* programme where presenter Sam Leitch told everyone, 'It's League Cup Final day at Hampden where Celtic meet Partick Thistle, who have no chance.'

No, we missed that as we were heading to my grandma's house at that same time, having arranged to pop in on our way to the game. She was quite chuffed we were going to honour my grandad's memory and handed over his old Thistle scarf for me to wear.

'He'll be looking out for you, so mind and keep it on,' she said as we waved goodbye.

So that's how I found myself in the covered end at Hampden that day holding aloft a Thistle scarf as the goals rained in. The fans around us could hardly believe what was happening.

Maybe we all should have. The number one single at that time was Rod Stewart's 'Reason To Believe', a double A-side with 'Maggie May'. Surely that was an omen for one of the greatest upsets in Scottish football.

My abiding memory of the final was turning towards my dad at full time amid the bedlam and seeing him with the biggest of big grins on his face. He looked at me silently and then raised his eyes to the skies above Hampden.

I knew what he meant. Grandad had been looking out for us.

IAN JACKSON

I walked to the game with my school-mates Lovatt Fraser and Kenny Reid from Mansewood on the Southside. I had decided that my tattered and chewed scarf should accompany me as opposed to the scarf emblazoned 'Scottish Cup Winners 20-21' my father had recently purchased for me. The scarf got progressively more gnawed as the second half progressed.

We floated home dancing, singing and pouring Irn-Bru over each other. A slight detour was needed at one point when a kindly gent informed us there was a gang of drunken, angry Celtic supporters a short distance ahead.

I spent the next two days visiting the newsagent to purchase any newspaper I thought may have a match report in it. I even got a copy of *Sporting Life* only to find it only concerned horse racing!

I've still got all the now dog-eared reports. The scarf lives on. Never got sewn up – I repaired it with a stapler. I chew it less now.

TOMMY DICKSON

I was 16 years old in October 1971 and went to the match with a couple of my friends, my dad and his best pal. We started the day by walking from Ruchill, where we lived at that time, into the 'toon', for a cup final breakfast in the Woolworths cafeteria in Argyle Street. Despite the difference in our generations, the five of us were all as high as kites, like a bunch of weans at Christmas.

I knew my dad was so proud and excited to be going to see the Jags play in a cup final along with his only son. After being fed and watered for the day we made our way through the Southside of the city to Hampden where we had shared some great memories of following the national team in magnificent crowds of 134,000 on a regular basis.

My dad had managed to obtain five tickets for the North Stand which sat high above the large terracing. Our seats were right on the halfway line, one of the best views you could have. There was no segregation and fans of both Thistle and Celtic were mingling quite happily especially in the centre of the stand. There was a buzz of excitement as kick-off drew closer. It was also a time when you could take a 'carry-oot' into a match, and my dad and his pal had picked up some refreshments on the way.

Just before the game started my dad pulled a half bottle of whisky from his pocket and said to his pal, 'We'll have a half for every goal the Jags score the day,' raising some laughs all around!

A Celtic fan sitting in the row in front of us turned around and said, 'Haw, big yin, you'll being going hame sober then.' More laughs!

Just before half-time, with the Jags 4-0 up, my dad tapped the Celtic fan on the shoulder. Holding the empty whisky bottle upside down and shaking it over the Celtic fan's head, my dad said, 'Haw, wee man, do you fancy going down to Haddows at half-time and getting me another bottle for the second half?' Hilarity all around!

To be fair to the Celtic fan, he turned around and shook my dad's hand and said, 'Fair enough, big yin, I think I'll get a bottle for myself, to drown my sorrows.'

A memory that I cherish above all others, I got to watch the Jags in a cup final. 'wae ma Da'.

MICK LEE

The 1971 Scottish League Cup Final was my first Partick Thistle game and, in fact my first Scottish club game. However, I was not a child but a 21-year-old student. This is how it came about.

I was born in Newcastle-upon-Tyne, I moved to Blackpool when I was two and then to Essex when I was six. My dad was a lifelong Newcastle United supporter, and he used to take me to see them play whenever they came to the London area. With school friends I would go and see first Romford FC in the Southern League, then West Ham in the First Division, but I never felt a full connection to them as I did to Newcastle.

In 1969 I gained a place at Glasgow School of Art and moved to the city. If I had been tempted to go to see club football it would probably have been Celtic because of the type of football they played, but I soon became aware of the baggage attached to the two big Glasgow teams and avoided both. There were a few Jags supporters on my course, and they tried to persuade me and a couple of other English exiles to go and see them, but we resisted. However, in 1971 their promise of exciting football that had got them promoted, including a couple of wingers, finally persuaded us when they made the final. The three of us, myself, Mike and Raj, took our place in the north enclosure and prepared for the worst. What followed needs no description from me, but we were hooked! Even subsequent maulings from Aberdeen and Celtic (again) shortly afterwards couldn't put us off. I even got invited to a party by a girl I fancied on the evening of the final and became the centre of attention when others found out I 'had been there'! The end of a perfect day.

Raj eventually moved back to England, but Mike and I stuck with it through good times and bad; promotions and relegations, cup semis and boring 0-0 draws, Save the Jags and everything else. I was a ground season ticket for quite a few years until it stopped being cost effective, and became a season ticket holder again on our last promotion to the Premiership which I have renewed ever since. My two daughters don't really have an interest in football, but both were proud to say they supported the Jags at school, and both came along to Firhill to do their bit for Save the Jags. One of them even married a Jags supporter!

It's probably going too far to say that going to the final changed my life, but it would be very different if I hadn't gone.

GERRY SHERIDAN

I was first taken to Firhill in the 1950s by my dad and uncle Tommy, who would lift me on to a crush barrier to watch the match. We lived in Ruchill at that time and it was only a short walk over the park to bring us to Firhill. I was too young to take it all in but my memory of that time is of the huge crowds.

In 1961 when I was 12 years old, I started going with my pal Jim Edmistone. We became hooked on Thistle and attended almost every home game, paying one shilling and sixpence or 'wan an a tanner' as they used to say, at the boys' gate. At age 13, I started going to away games as well with another pal John Toal and we travelled on the Whiteinch supporters' bus. My favourite players were Davie McParland, Neil Duffy, Sandy Brown and Billy Hainey to name a few.

In April 1971, I joined the merchant ship M.V. *Lossiebank* as an engineer and in October that year, we found ourselves docked in Sydney, Australia. There were three Jags fans on the ship – myself, Roddy the second engineer and Bob the radio officer. As the day of the cup final drew ever closer, the three of us agreed that with McParland in charge we were in with a chance, because as a skilful player, Davie had always given 100 per cent effort in every match he played and we felt that as a manager, his players would be left in no doubt of what he expected from them.

We also felt that this was a Thistle team that contained a good blend of skill, youth and experience. Other members of the crew wished us luck, adding, 'Ye'll need it.'

The big day arrived and, at the time of the match, I was on duty in the engine room and had been busy working when the phone at the telegraph rang loudly. I answered 'engine room' thinking I was going to be asked to start another generator, but it was Bob and he shouted down the line, 'It's half-time at Hampden and Thistle are up 4-0.'

Now if he had said 1-0 or even 2-0, I would have believed it. But for Thistle to be up 4-0 at half-time against a Celtic side who were being described in the media as one of the best in Europe, it seemed a wee bit far-fetched, so I said 'aye right,' thinking it was a wind-up and went back to work.

At the end of my watch, I came up from the engine room to take a shower when I heard music and laughter coming from the lounge of Roddy's large cabin. I walked up to his open cabin door to find that a party was in full swing and that's when it dawned on me that we had won the cup. Roddy and Bob saw me standing at the cabin door in my boiler suit and started shouting, 'We've done it, we've won the League Cup.'

A drink was thrust into my hand as I asked them the final score. 'Four-one for Thistle,' I was told, as other members of the crew joined us and we all raised our glasses in a toast to a great victory.

Since that famous time, I went on to set up and run the Livingston Partick Thistle Supporters' Club. My son William became DJ/announcer at Firhill and also provided the entertainment at player of the year functions. William now lives in Ireland but comes over for matches whenever he can. My dad Tommy attended his last Thistle match at age 92 and sadly passed away a year later. Our family tradition of supporting Thistle carries on through the generations and I still go to Firhill with my other son Craig, his lovely wife Mandy and my grandchildren Eireann and Ciaran and we are always joined by friends.

As a lifelong supporter, I live in hope of actually being there when Thistle next go up to lift a major cup.

DOUGLAS DAVIDSON

My family hail from Maryhill and I was taken along to Firhill and a few away games since I was about ten years old, my heroes of the day being guys like Tommy Ewing and Davie McParland. These were the days when there were 'football specials' – full trains of Thistle fans bound for places like Dunfermline in 1966 for a cup match.

In season 1970, instead of the usual few outstanding players, we had a full team of them, from Rough in goals to Lawrie on the left wing. I attended every match, home and away that season, once being left behind in Methil after a midweek match by the north-west supporters' bus and having to take a taxi back to Glasgow. Much to the dismay of my parents who had to foot the bill.

The cup final in October 1971 followed a great start to the season including a famous victory over Rangers, and an amazing fightback over two legs against St. Johnstone. So I thought we had a chance against Celtic. My memory of that day is coming out of Hampden where the newspaper vendors were already selling the special edition with 'photos of the champions' as they were calling out. My other memory is getting roughed up by some Celtic supporters at the bus stop in Renfrew Street on the way home. All in all a memorable day.

The following week we chartered a bus from Bearsden, which was full, and went to Aberdeen where unfortunately we lost 7-2. My memory of that match was the Thistle team getting a guard of honour with the whole of Pittodrie rising to them.

DAVID HORNSBY

The final was seen by many as a foregone conclusion but I recall thinking we had a real chance as we had some very good, confident, young players.

It was raining as we made our way to Hampden and out tickets were for the west terracing or 'Rangers End'. There were Thistle fans and Celtic supporters in close proximity but there was no bad feeling or trouble.

First, captain Alex Rae put us ahead with a volley followed by a good goal from Bobby Lawrie. Then Denis McQuade made it 3-0 and the scoring wasn't over as Jimmy Bone made the half-time scoreline 4-0.

The second half saw Celtic coming at the Jags hard in the first 20 minutes but Thistle also had chances to increase their tally.

Alan Rough was magnificent and was only beaten once. Long before the end Celtic were a beaten side and the sound of 'Thistle! Thistle! Thistle!' being sung around the ground was deafening.

When Alex Rae lifted the gleaming trophy I was in dreamland!

At 17 years of age I knew life would never be better for me as a Thistle fan. Almost 50 years on it never has been!

IAN CURRIE

I attended the game as a nine year-old with my twin brother David, older brother Alan and my dad and grandad, both lifelong Thistle fans. I am pretty sure my grandad attended the cup final victory in 1921.

Tickets for the final were arranged with my uncle, Jim Rutherford, who was club secretary at Queen's Park for many years.

The day started with a journey through from family home in Gullane to pick up my grandad in Possilpark and then down in good time to Hampden for the match.

Looking back on the day it must have been difficult for my dad as I was supporting the Jags and my twin brother supporting Celtic. In addition to managing these sensitivities my grandfather was blind. I remember his excitement attending the final with his family and young grandchildren.

Little were we to know what was to happen later!

We arrived, met our uncle and, full of excitement, went to our seats in the main stand.

The game kicked off and the plan was for my dad to do a running commentary for my grandad. This started well but after 36 minutes when the fourth goal went in I recall my dad being unable to describe what was actually happening to my grandfather who was struggling to keep up with the fact we were 4-0 up at that time to a team fielding many Lisbon Lions. My dad was also comforting my crying twin brother at the same time as he was overjoyed to see his beloved team winning a final.

I recall the celebration at the final whistle, watching Alex Rae lifting the cup, and left elated to drop my grandad back home with a celebratory 'hauf and hauf'. We left him singing and headed back home tired and elated.

What an unbelievable achievement. I'm proud to say I was there; a lifelong commitment was cemented on that day. I'm proud also to say that my own sons Michael and Stuart have followed the family tradition as fourth-generation Jags fans.

SANDY BOYD

My special memory of the 1971 cup final involves three generations of my family. Myself, my dad and my grandfather.

On the day my grandfather had to work and was pretty gutted to be missing the game. My dad was going with his uncle and they, like most at the game, were pretty stunned by the scoreline and knew they were witnessing something special.

After the celebrations they made their way out and both spotted my grandad working and jumped out in front of him dancing and waving scarves in the air! The only problem was my grandad was a coach driver and had a bus full of Celtic supporters, taking them home, who were all asking him if he knew them. 'Never seen them before in my life,' he told them.

Little did they know it was his son and his brother.

We lived at the time in Murano Street next to Firhill and on hearing the result my mum decided to walk me down in my pram (I was two) to greet the players on their return. Luckily for me, though not so much the players, someone had forgotten the keys to the ground so while we all waited we got our pics taken with the players. A great memento of a great day. And I blame this for my continued love of the Jags to this day.

TOM STOKES

In 1971 I was in my third year at Paisley College and I was staying in the halls of residence. I was the only known Jags fan in the halls.

Saturday, 23 October started as most Saturdays did, with a college football match away somewhere in Glasgow. The college scarf is very dark blue with a red and yellow stripe so our team colours were yellow tops with red shorts. I can't remember the score. In the afternoon after dropping off my football gear, it was off to Hampden. The first half was like a dream but, like most of the crowd, the second half was nervy – could we hold on to our 4-0 lead?

After the game I had just enough time to get back to Paisley in time for tea in the college canteen. As I walked in slightly late, everyone stood up and cheered. You would have thought that I had won the cup myself.

However, there was one young lady there who was wondering who I was and why the cheer. Two weeks later we were going out together and married the next September. We still are.

Quite a day to remember.

JIM HENDRY

Sitting in the press box at Firs Park, reporting for the *Falkirk Herald* as East Stirlingshire took on Dumbarton in the Scottish Second Division, events at Hampden were not foremost on my mind until a colleague's utterance of the by-now familiar refrain, 'You'll never guess the half-time score at Hampden.'

In these pre-internet, pre-Jeff Stelling days, freelance journalist and Thistle sympathiser George Findlay was the man delivering the breaking news as he phoned over his first-half copy to the *Pink Times* in Glasgow. It was, in football terms, the definitive JFK moment ... what a sensation indeed.

As a non-Old Firm supporter, any team that bloodied the nose of either of the big two was all right in my book so admiration for the Firhill heroes was off the scale that weekend. And, as a Dundee FC diehard, fate decreed that me and my likes would be the first to show our appreciation when Thistle called into Dens the following midweek.

Having just days earlier passed my driving test, the road and the miles on that foggy evening proved to be, ahem, let's just say it was an interesting journey.

And did my admiration for Thistle prevail? Not a chance. Ten thousand Dark Blues turned up to show our appreciation to Scottish football's men of the moment and how did they thank us?

Thistle killed the game stone dead with an ultra-defensive show and Alan Rough almost broke his back fielding back-passes from start to finish. After this shocker of a goalless draw, it's fair to say that Thistle had tumbled off the pedestal and normal service had been resumed.

IAN RICHARDSON

I remember very well going to Hampden Park on 23 October 1971 with my friend Harry who was a keen Thistle fan. Although I am a Hearts fan, Partick Thistle was considered to be my Glasgow team. After my sons were born, on occasions I took them along to Firhill and one of them became a Thistle fan and was a Thistle mascot sometime later.

I lived in Kings Park so Harry and I walked to Hampden enjoying the excitement of the crowds all heading to the League Cup Final. We noticed a Mini car trying to get into a space smaller than it was. Easily remedied! Some supporters lifted the car in the front of the space and moved it as far forward as it could go, then lifted the Mini into the now slightly bigger space – job done! We arrived at Hampden and made our way to the East End terracing and waited for the match to begin.

Thistle scored once, then a second goal against Celtic. This was followed by Thistle scoring a third then a fourth, all in the first half. What a match! Thistle fans were on an all-time high at half-time. Midway through the second half saw Celtic scoring a consolation goal, and the game ended 4-1 for Thistle.

Thistle had played very well and the fans were delighted to see them picking up the cup.

Harry and I walked home, discussing the goals and how well Thistle had played and how Alan Rough kept Celtic at bay.

Harry, myself and our wives went out for a meal at night to celebrate. During our meal we saw a 'weel kent' Celtic player at the bar, maybe drowning his sorrows!

KEVIN McCLUSKEY

When I hear people say they have lived a life with no regrets I'm not sure I believe them because I certainly can't say that. One of my biggest regrets was not being at Hampden on that incredible day in October 1971.

I was born in Maryhill and had been taken to a few Thistle matches by my grandfather when I was much younger and duly became a Thistle fan. For my 14 birthday in August 1971 I had got myself a season ticket – what a time to become serious about Thistle. An early-season 3-2 defeat of Rangers. And so it began!

By the time of the final I had come to realise I wasn't going to get there. I went to the matches on my own, had my own seat in the stand, loved everything about the matches, the atmosphere around them, the smell of Bovril and the pies. It was all great but I had no connection with the people around me – they were so much older than I was!

Anyway, knowing that as a quiet, shy 14-year-old the task of organising a ticket for the final was beyond my capability I resigned myself to listening to the match on the radio.

An obvious problem with the plan was that at that time BBC Scotland only broadcast the second half of a Saturday match. So there I was that Saturday afternoon, tuning in up in my bedroom.

The broadcaster began by saying he was taking us back to four incidents in the first half and I thought, 'Oh no, we're 4-0 down!' But no, the first 'incident' is a

Thistle attack and a goal.

'Okay, so it's only 3-1, not bad,' I thought.

The second 'incident' is another Thistle attack and goal.

'Two-two. That's great!'

The third 'incident' and it's another Thistle attack and goal.

'My God! We're 3-1 up! This is incredible!'

But it gets even better. Fourth 'incident' yet another Thistle attack and goal. I nearly hit the roof.

I ran down the stairs.

'Four-nil, 4-0! It's unbelievable! We're 4-0 up at half-time!'

While my delight was not necessarily shared by all at home there was some element of being pleased for me.

Of course, we went on to win 4-1 and I will never forget the members of that team, many of whom left within a relatively short time.

I have lived in Cork for over 30 years but I try to get back for a few Thistle games each year.

As I said at the start – that day is one that I would certainly love to be able to change for myself, if that were possible! But, alas, some lives do have regrets!

IAIN McIVER

This was my FIFTH visit to Hampden to watch Thistle in a League Cup Final. A 3-2 loss to East Fife in 1953, a 3-0 loss to Celtic in a replay after a 0-0 draw in 1956 and a 5-1 hammering by Hearts in 1958 wasn't a great record to help me build up my hopes! The 3-0 defeat to Celtic in 1956 was a particularly painful experience in more ways than one. In order to attend a weekday afternoon replay, a choice had to be made between football and school. Returning to Hillhead High School the following morning, those of us who had preferred the match were swiftly belted for our unauthorised absence.

Now back to 1971. Recently promoted Thistle were up against a Celtic team which had reached the European Cup Final for a second time in the previous year and were of course huge favourites. Accompanied by my wife Joyce and my father (a Rangers supporter!), I took my seat in the old South Stand. Our seats were level with the 18-yard line at the Mount Florida end, so provided a fantastic view of what was to follow, especially in that amazing first half.

On turning round prior to the kick-off, I discovered that the row behind was occupied by several priests.

After Thistle's first goal I felt a tap on the shoulder and a friendly smiling face congratulated me on the promising start, no doubt assuming that this would be our consolation goal before the anticipated onslaught. As goals two, three and four hit the net there were no further taps on the shoulder and when I turned round at half-time the seats were empty!

Talk about being excited. My wife tells me that she thought I was going to have a heart attack as each succeeding goal was scored, and the unbelievable first half materialised in front of us. Despite the 4-0 lead, the second half was still a nail biter with the vision of a 5-4 defeat never far away. Fortunately Celtic's consolation goal was the only minor fright as Thistle held on comfortably until the final whistle. The next day I bought about every Sunday paper I could find in order to enjoy the moment to the full.

Thistle 'celebrated' the following week with a 0-0 draw at Dens Park followed by a 7-2 defeat to Aberdeen at Pittodrie. Yes! Life as a Thistle fan was soon back to normal!

I've still got my programme (price 5p) which contained an interesting feature on the history of the cup from its inception in 1946. The first goal scored in the final would be the 100th cup final goal, so well done Alex Rae. The article suggested that this goal might come from Celtic's Lou Macari, Kenny Dalglish, Billy McNeil (didn't play) or even Jimmy Johnstone!

Only Jimmy Bone of Thistle got a mention, so who would have guessed he would score goal number 103!

DAVID MACKAY

In 1971 I was a junior officer in the Parachute Regiment. My battalion, 3 PARA, was taking part in a large training exercise. Over 5,000 men and vehicles had parachuted on to Salisbury Plain at the beginning of the week. The work was hard and the weather was cold and wet. Amazingly, my boss, who knew nothing about football, had a soft spot for Thistle – he was intrigued by the name. He gave me 36 hours' leave for the final.

My eight-hour journey to Scotland involved travelling in the back of an Army truck, a bus to Heathrow and then a plane to Glasgow.

My dad and I set off for the game next day. He had missed the 1921 Scottish Cup Final as he was at sea training school at that time and was aboard an Anchor Line ship in New York in 1929. Perhaps this would be the day he could see the Jags win a major trophy. It was! I looked at my lovely dad at the end and all he said was, 'Well, well, good result.'

That evening I boarded a plane at Glasgow Airport to Heathrow and made my way back to Aldershot. At 6am the next day I was on board a military plane at Farnborough and rejoined the exercise by parachute.

My abiding memory of the day is my dad's quiet smile of satisfaction.

ACKNOWLEDGEMENTS

It is all Hugh MacDonald's fault. Who would have thought that a quick lunch in Raffaelle's Italian restaurant in Bearsden would have resulted in this book? It was Hugh's throwaway comment about it being 'a big year for your club' that started me on this journey. I can't thank Hugh enough for giving me the idea and for being at the end of a phone for a chat or a piece of advice.

Stuart Deans has been another constant source of support and I thank him for being generous with his time and for his help. The cuttings and old newspaper clippings he was able to supply were a goldmine of information that I was able to tap into.

Then there are the huge number of Thistle fans who responded with their memories of that day in 1971. People such as Douglas Davidson in Kuala Lumpur or David Hornsby who not only supplied words but some quite splendid caricatures of the players as well, or Susan Watson whose collection of Thistle memorabilia has to be seen to be believed. To each and every one of them who took the time to send me their story I say thank you. Their passion for Partick Thistle remains undiminished by the passage of time.

To Davie McParland's daughter Yvonne who gave up her time to talk to me about her father – a man who holds an extra special place in her heart.

And talk of family brings me to my own. To Siobhan, Joe, Sam and Eve and to Marnie the dog. No husband or father could ask for any better. When I was at my lowest ebb they were there to pick me up and show me that being knocked down is not failure, failure is not getting back up.

To all my friends, too many to name here, who have been so supportive and helpful, you know who you are. To my brother Lewis for his help and guidance over the years. And to my younger brother Tony – never forgotten.

To Jim McCann and all at SNS for their help in sourcing pictures. To Michelle Grainger at publishers JMD Media.

And finally a special thanks to Alan, John, Alex, Ronnie, Jackie, Hugh, Denis, Jimmy, Frank, Alex, Bobby and John, and of course to Davie.

Never forget – Maryhill, is wonderful!

BV - #0059 - 041121 - C0 - 234/156/9 - PB - 9781780916255 - Matt Lamination